TIMES TABLES TABLES GAMES for Clever Kids

Puzzles and solutions
by Dr Gareth Moore

B.Sc (Hons) M.Phil Ph.D

Illustrations and cover
artwork by Chris Dickason

Designed by Zoe Bradley

Edited by Frances Evans

Cover Design by Angie Allison

Educational Consultancy by Paul Wrangles

TIMES TABLES GAMES for Clever Kids

BUSTER BOOKS

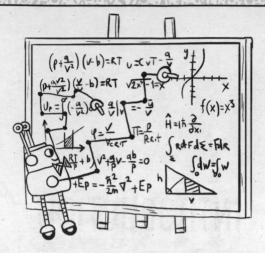

First published in Great Britain in 2018 by Buster Books,
an imprint of Michael O'Mara Books Limited,
9 Lion Yard, Tremadoc Road, London SW4 7NQ

W www.mombooks.com/buster
f Buster Books
@BusterBooks
@buster_books

Clever Kids is a trade mark of Michael O'Mara Books Limited.

Puzzles and solutions © Gareth Moore 2018

Illustrations and layouts © Buster Books 2018

A CIP catalogue record for this book is available from the British Library.

ISBN: 978-1-78055-562-1

11 13 15 17 19 20 18 16 14 12

This product is made of material from well-managed, FSC®-certified
forests and other controlled sources. The manufacturing processes conform
to the environmental regulations of the country of origin.

Printed and bound in October 2023 by
CPI Group (UK) Ltd, Croydon, CR0 4YY.

MIX
Paper | Supporting
responsible forestry
FSC® C171272

INTRODUCTION

Are you ready for a challenge? This book contains over 100 times-tables games, which are designed to put your multiplication skills to the test. Each game can be tackled on its own and you only need to know your 1 to 12 times tables. Sometimes you might think that you need to multiply numbers larger than 12, but there is always a way to solve each problem without doing so.

At the top of every page, there is a space for you to write how much time it took you to complete each game. Don't be afraid to make notes on the pages – this can be a good tactic to help you keep track of your thoughts. There are some blank pages at the back of the book that you can use for working out your answers.

Read the simple instructions on each page before tackling a game. If you get stuck, read the instructions again in case there's something you missed. Work in pencil so you can rub things out and have another try.

If you are still stuck, you could also try asking an adult, although did you know that your brain is actually much more powerful than a grown-up's? When you get older, your brain will get rid of lots of bits of information it thinks it doesn't need any more, which means you might be better at solving these games than older people are.

If you're **REALLY** stuck, have a peek at the answers at the back of the book, and then try to work out how you could have got to that solution yourself.

Now, good luck and have fun!

Here is the full 1 to 12 times-tables grid. This grid
is all you will need for every game in the book!

×	1	2	3	4	5	6	7	8	9	10	11	12
1	1	2	3	4	5	6	7	8	9	10	11	12
2	2	4	6	8	10	12	14	16	18	20	22	24
3	3	6	9	12	15	18	21	24	27	30	33	36
4	4	8	12	16	20	24	28	32	36	40	44	48
5	5	10	15	20	25	30	35	40	45	50	55	60
6	6	12	18	24	30	36	42	48	54	60	66	72
7	7	14	21	28	35	42	49	56	63	70	77	84
8	8	16	24	32	40	48	56	64	72	80	88	96
9	9	18	27	36	45	54	63	72	81	90	99	108
10	10	20	30	40	50	60	70	80	90	100	110	120
11	11	22	33	44	55	66	77	88	99	110	121	132
12	12	24	36	48	60	72	84	96	108	120	132	144

Introducing the Multiplication Master:
Gareth Moore, B.Sc (Hons) M.Phil Ph.D

Dr Gareth Moore is an Ace Puzzler,
and author of lots of puzzle and
brain-training books.

He created an online brain-training
site called BrainedUp.com, and runs an
online puzzle site called PuzzleMix.com.
Gareth has a Ph.D from the University of
Cambridge, where he taught machines
to understand spoken English.

These robots are charging their electric hovercars. Can you work out how much energy each car needs by completing these calculations?

Begin with the number at the START of each calculation, then multiply it by each number in the sequence until you reach the end. Write your answer in the empty box on the cars. See if you can do all the maths in your head, without making any written notes.

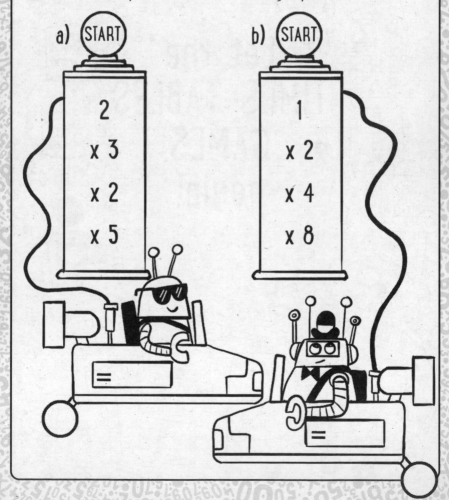

a) START

2

x 3

x 2

x 5

b) START

1

x 2

x 4

x 8

Complete each of these multiplication calculations and then find them hidden in the grid below. The calculations can be written in any direction, including diagonally, and may read either forwards or backwards (don't get confused by the backwards ones!). One is solved for you already as an example: 4 × 5 = 20

$4 \times 5 = 20$　　　$3 \times \_ = 12$

$1 \times \_ = 4$　　　$3 \times 5 = \_\_$

$\_ \times 5 = 5$　　　$\_ \times 4 = 16$

$2 \times \_ = 10$　　　$5 \times 3 = \_\_$

$\_ \times 2 = 6$　　　$5 \times \_ = 25$

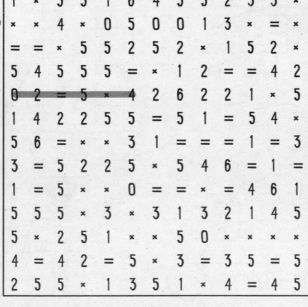

1	×	5	5	1	6	4	5	5	2	3	3	×
×	×	4	×	0	5	0	0	1	3	×	=	×
=	=	×	5	5	2	5	2	×	1	5	2	×
5	4	5	5	5	=	×	1	2	=	=	4	2
0	2	=	5	×	4	2	6	2	2	1	×	5
1	4	2	2	5	5	=	5	1	=	5	4	×
5	6	=	×	×	3	1	=	=	=	1	=	3
3	=	5	2	2	5	×	5	4	6	=	1	=
1	=	5	×	×	0	=	=	×	=	4	6	1
5	5	5	×	3	×	3	1	3	2	1	4	5
5	×	2	5	1	×	×	5	0	×	×	×	×
4	=	4	2	=	5	×	3	=	3	5	=	5
2	5	5	×	1	3	5	1	×	4	=	4	5

Can you fill in the missing numbers in each of these number triangles, so that every square and circle contains a number? Each square should contain the result of multiplying the two circled numbers on either side of it.

In this example 2 x 9 = 18,
9 x 7 = 63 and 2 x 7 = 14

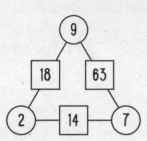

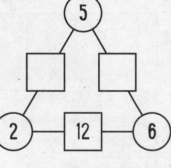

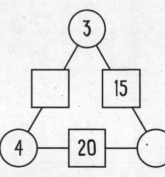

Look at these picture equations. Can you work out the value of each of the following tools? No tool has a value higher than 12.

🪛 x 🔨 x 🔧 = 40

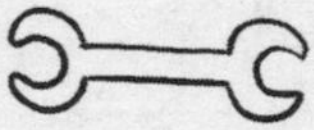

🔧 x 🪛 = 10

🪛 x 🪛 = 4

Write your answers here:

🪛 = ...

🔨 = ...

🔧 = ...

Can you conquer these number pyramids? Write a number in each empty block so that every block contains a number equal to the product of the two numbers directly beneath it.

Take a look at this completed example to see how it works:

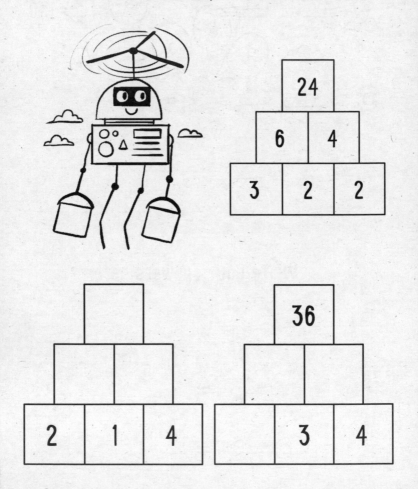

This robot has bought a bunch of balloons and each one has a different number painted on it.

Can you work out which balloons you need to burst so that the remaining numbers multiply together to form each of the following totals? For example, you could form a total of 10 by bursting all the balloons except 5 and 2, since 5 x 2 = 10. You can leave more than two balloons to reach your answer.

Write your answers here:

a) 15 = ...

b) 24 = ...

c) 36 = ...

d) 60 = ...

TIMES-TABLES GAME 7 →

Each of these robot chains is made up of the values in a times table. Work out which times tables are displayed and then write the missing values in the spaces on the robots to complete the sequences. Begin with the number at the START of each robot chain, then follow the arrows in turn.

a)

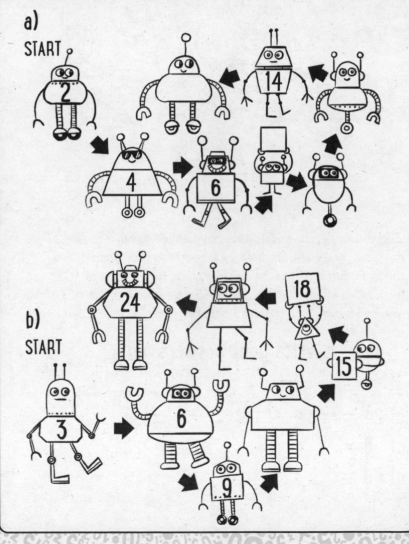

START

2 → 4 → 6 → ... → ... → ... → 14 → ...

b)

START

3 → 6 → 9 → ... → 15 → 18 → ... → 24

c)
START

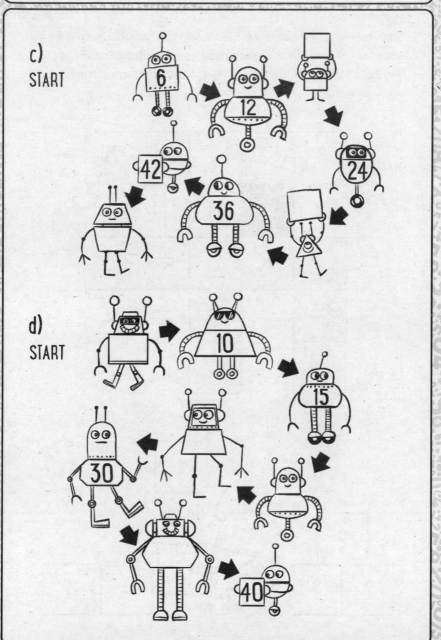

Can you place the numbers 2, 3, 4 and 6 once each into the empty squares to solve these mathematical calculations? Two calculations read from left to right and two read from top to bottom.

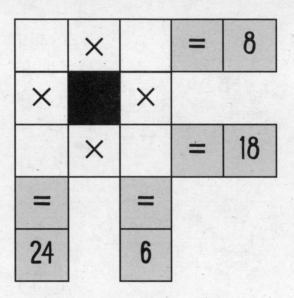

Help this artistic robot complete his masterpiece. Colour in the shapes in the puzzle below according to the following rules, to reveal a hidden picture.

Multiples of:

3 = red
4 = blue
5 = green
7 = yellow
11 = orange

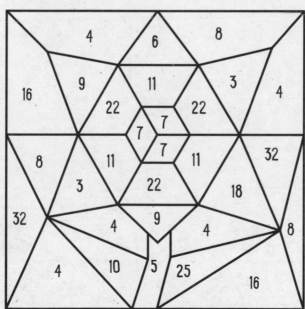

This next puzzle is designed to really put your knowledge of the 1 to 12 times tables to the test! The same digit is missing from all of the following numbers. If that digit was added back in then all the numbers would be products from the times tables. The numbers must come from the 1 to 12 times tables, from 1 x 1 to 12 x 12.

For example, if you had 14_ and _0 then the missing digit would be 4 because 144 and 40 are both products in the times tables (144 is the product of 12 x 12 and 40 is the product of 5 x 8 or 8 x 5 and 4 x 10 or 10 x 4).

Which digit is missing from the following times-tables products?

_1

4_

2_

1_

8_

_4

A section of the times-tables grid is displayed on this robot, but some of the values are missing. Can you work out what the sequences are and fill in all the numbers? If you need a reminder, you can always turn back to the grid in the introduction, but try to fill it in from memory first. The first line has been done for you.

To solve these calcudoku puzzles, place the numbers 1 to 3 once each into every row and column. You must place these numbers so that the values in each bold-lined region of grid squares multiply to give the small number printed in the top left-hand corner of the region.

This finished puzzle shows you how it works:

The numbers in each bold segment multiply together to equal the small number in the corner. For instance, 1 x 2 x 3 = 6 and 2 x 3 = 6 in these bold segments.

3	6 1	6 2
2 1	2	3
2	3	1

Puzzle 1

2		3
6		
2	3	

Puzzle 2

2		6
3	3	
	2	

Help this robot find a route through the maze to meet her friend on the other side. The route must only pass over numbers that are all in the same times table as one another. For example, it could cross over 3, 6, 12 and 15, as these are all in the 3 times table, but it could not then cross over a 4, or any other number not in the 3 times table.

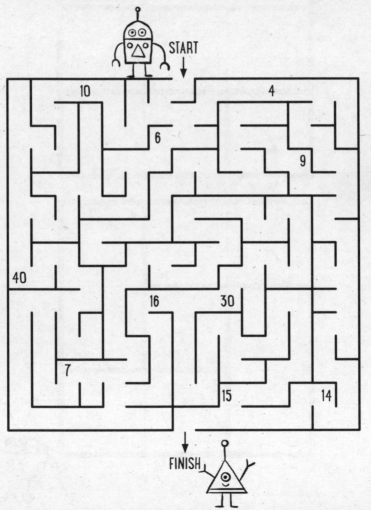

Can you form the products below by choosing one number from each ring on this dartboard and then multiplying them together?

For example, you could form a product of 14 by picking 2 from the inner ring and 7 from the outer ring.

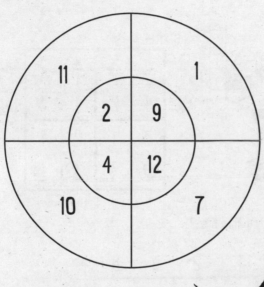

Products:

20 = ...

40 = ...

84 = ...

To solve this frame sudoku puzzle, place the numbers 1 to 4 once each into every row, column and bold-lined 2x2 box. The numbers outside the grid tell you the product of the two nearest numbers in the corresponding row or column.

Here's a finished example:

For instance, 4 x 2 = 8 and 3 x 2 = 6

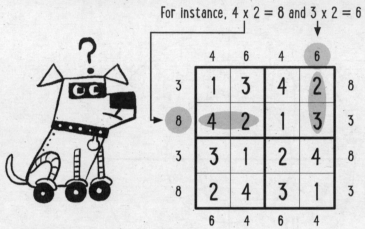

Now try this puzzle:

	12	2	3	8	
6			1		**4**
4		1			**6**
6			4		**4**
4		4			**6**
	2	12	8	3	

Can you place each of the following numbers into the columns below, so that every column contains two numbers? Be careful, as some numbers will fit into more than one column but there is only one way of fitting two numbers into each column.

TWO MULTIPLES OF 3	TWO MULTIPLES OF 4	TWO MULTIPLES OF 6

Can you solve these written multiplication puzzles?

a) Tina has three hats and then goes shopping to buy some more. Now she has twice the number of hats that she had to start with. However, she then gives away a third of her hats. How many hats does she have left?

Answer: ....

b) This robot has two children under the age of 13 and neither of them are the same age. The product of the children's ages is 16. How old is each child?

Answer: ....and................

Complete this dot-to-dot puzzle by joining multiples of 3 in increasing numerical order to reveal something you can see at night. Ignore any numbers that are not multiples of 3.

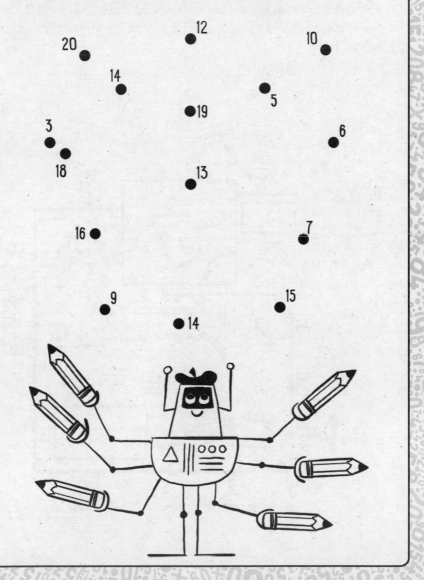

Can you work out the result of the calculations in these mathematical machines? Begin with the number at the START of each sequence, then complete the calculations in order until you reach the end. Write your answer after the equals symbol. See if you can do all the maths in your head, without making any written notes.

a)
START

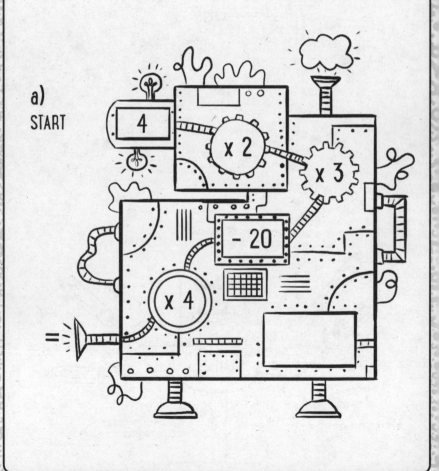

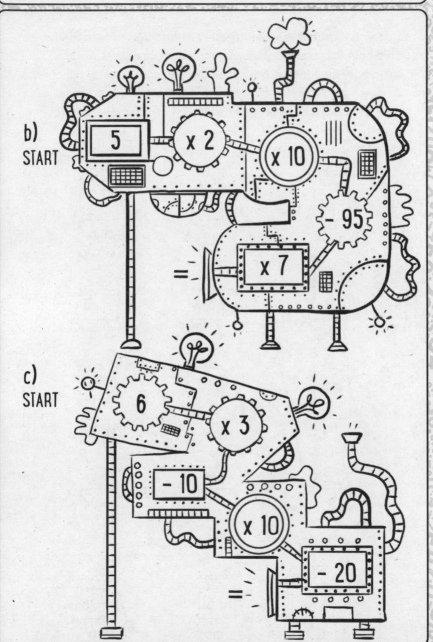

b) START

5 × 2 × 10 − 95 × 7 =

c) START

6 × 3 − 10 × 10 − 20 =

Can you draw lines to join the numbers in the first, second and third columns to create five correct multiplications? One has already been done to show you how the puzzle works, since 6 x 2 = 12. Be careful, as there is more than one way to create some products but there is only one way of using every robot exactly once each.

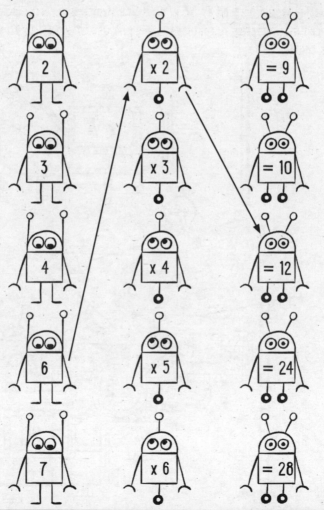

Three different digits, A, B and C, have been used to write down two multiplication calculations from the times tables. Can you work out the value of each digit? A digit is any number from 0 to 9 and they have the same value in both calculations.

For example, if you thought A = 5, B = 7 and C = 9, then the first calculation would be read as 57 x 59 = 579 (which is incorrect). No advanced mathematics is required – only the use of your 1 to 12 times tables.

$$AB \times AC = ABC$$
$$AA \times AA = ABA$$

Write your answers here:

A = ...

B = ...

C = ...

Look at these picture equations. Can you work out the value of each mini-bot? No mini-bot has a value higher than 12.

 x = **12**

 x = **24**

 x = **18**

Write your answers here:

 = ...

 = ...

 = ...

In each of the following calculations, there is one extra digit that shouldn't be there. Can you cross it out so that each calculation is correct?

For example, 12 x 4 = 8 can be fixed by crossing out 1 to leave 2 x 4 = 8.

a) 17 x 3 = 21

b) 12 x 54 = 60

c) 10 x 11 x 12 = 132

These robots have a square-shaped garden. They want to build a shed in the top-right corner of the garden. The part reserved for the shed is a square with an area of 4 m². This is shown on the plan below along with a further measurement.

Can you use these measurements to work out the total area of the garden? Write your answer in the space below. Remember, the area of a square is equal to its width times its height. This puzzle is designed to put your times-tables skills to the test in a new way, so don't worry if you find it tricky!

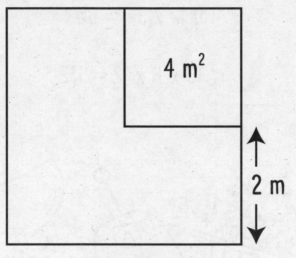

4 m²

2 m

The garden is:
.... m²

A section of the times-tables grid is displayed on this robot, but some of the values are missing. Can you work out what the sequences are and fill in all the numbers? If you need a reminder, you can always turn back to the grid in the introduction, but try to fill it in from memory first.

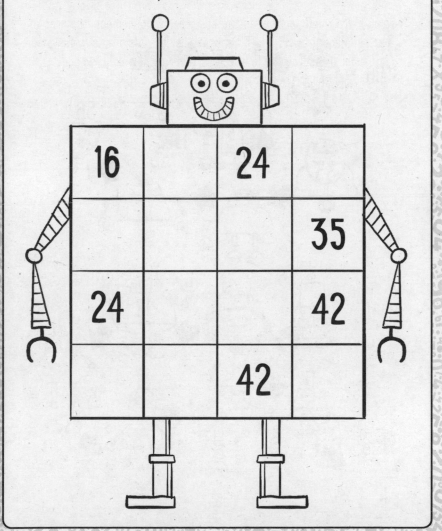

TIMES-TABLES GAME 26 →

Each of these robot chains is made up of the values in a times table. Work out which times tables are displayed and then write the missing values in the spaces on the robots to complete the sequences. Begin with the number at the START of each robot chain, then follow the arrows in turn.

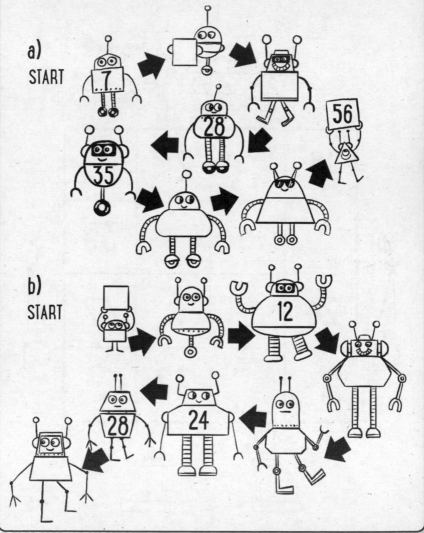

a)
START
7

28

35

56

b)
START

12

24

28

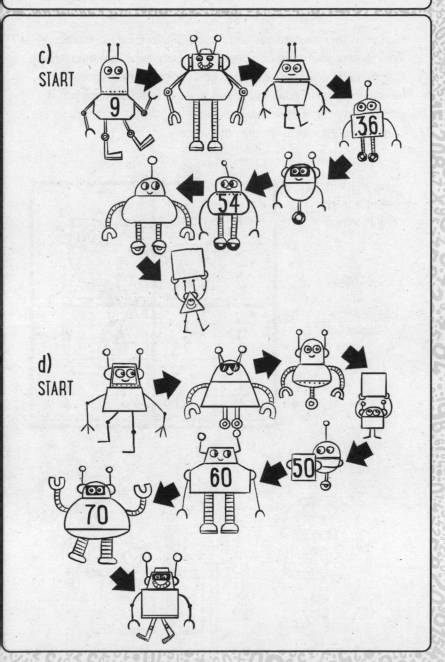

c)
START

d)
START

Can you crack the 'killer sudoku' puzzles on the opposite page? You need to place the numbers 1 to 4 once each into every row, column and bold-lined 2x2 box. Each dashed-line region also has a number printed in its top left-hand corner. To complete the puzzle correctly, all the numbers that you place in that region must multiply together to give this value.

Have a look at this example to see how it works:

For instance, in this dashed-line region, $4 \times 2 \times 1 = 8$ →

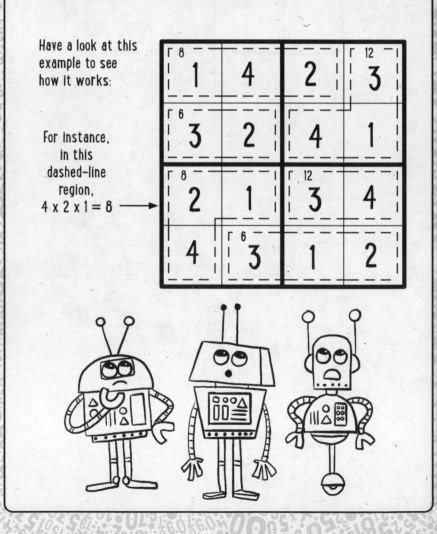

TIME ....

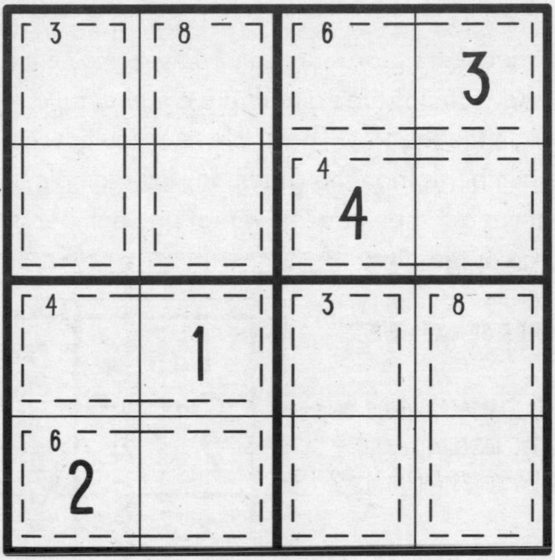

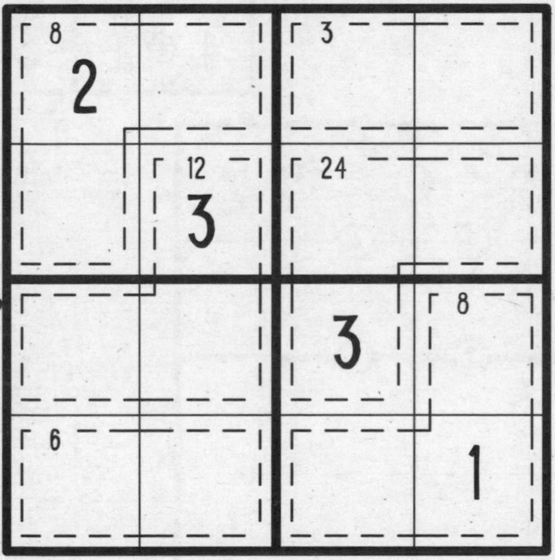

To solve the 'multiples' sudoku puzzle below, place the numbers 1 to 4 once each into every row, column and bold-lined box.

When two touching squares are joined by a small circled number, it shows that there's a multiple connection between the numbers in the squares. The circle tells you how many times larger one number is than the other. So, for example, if the circled contains a 3 then you know that one number is three times as large as the other.

Here's an example:

2 is twice as large as 1, for instance, and 4 is twice as large as 2

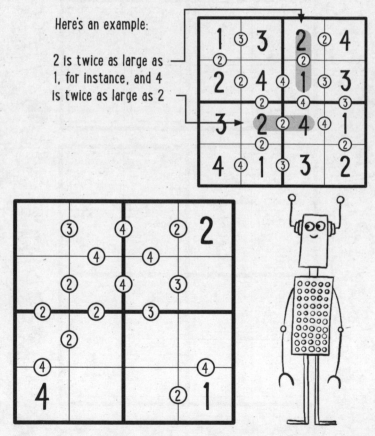

Complete each of these multiplication calculations and then find them hidden in the grid below. The calculations can be written in any direction, including diagonally, and may read either forwards or backwards (don't get confused by the backwards ones!). One is solved for you already as an example: $5 \times 4 = 20$

$5 \times 4 = 20$ $3 \times \_ = 18$

$1 \times \_ = 3$ $4 \times 2 = \_$

$2 \times 4 = \_$ $\_ \times 4 = 16$

$\_ \times 6 = 12$ $5 \times 3 = \_\_$

$2 \times \_ = 6$ $\_ \times 6 = 30$

$3 \times 3 = \_$ $\_ \times 4 = 24$

$3 \times 4 = \_\_$ $6 \times \_ = 36$

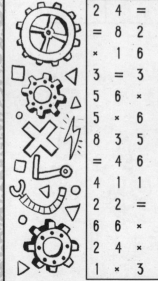

2	4	=	4	6	3	=	6	×	6	4	6	=
=	8	2	=	×	4	6	3	×	4	=	1	2
×	1	6	×	=	4	×	2	×	6	=	1	2
3	=	3	×	3	3	=	6	4	4	1	8	4
5	6	×	6	6	=	1	1	6	5	×	6	×
5	×	6	=	3	0	6	2	6	2	3	3	4
8	3	5	×	3	=	1	5	×	4	=	4	=
=	4	6	6	3	=	=	4	8	5	3	=	×
4	1	1	3	×	=	=	2	×	=	3	2	×
2	2	=	1	3	8	2	×	×	3	2	5	1
6	6	×	4	=	2	4	=	8	×	×	×	×
2	4	×	2	9	4	=	5	2	2	=	2	4
1	×	3	3	0	2	=	4	×	5	6	6	3

Can you conquer these number pyramids? Write a number in each empty block so that every block contains a number equal to the product of the two numbers directly beneath it.

To solve this frame sudoku puzzle, place 1 to 4 once each into every row, column and bold-lined 2x2 box. The numbers outside the grid tell you the product of the two nearest numbers in the corresponding row or column.

Have a look at this example to see how it works:

For instance, 2 x 3 = 6 and 4 x 2 = 8

	4	6	4	6	
3	1	3	4	2	8
8	4	2	1	3	3
3	3	1	2	4	8
8	2	4	3	1	3
	6	4	6	4	

	4	6	6	4	
12				1	2
2					12
2					12
12	3				2
	6	4	4	6	

Can you solve these written multiplication puzzles?

a) Sam's back garden is 5 metres wide x 4 metres long. A quarter of the garden is kept for a path and the other three-quarters are grassed over. If the grassed over area is rectangular, and each side is a whole number of metres in width and length, then what are the dimensions of the grassed area?

Answer: ....

b) Dina has four biscuits, which she carefully cuts in half. She now has double the number of biscuit pieces. If she then cuts all of the pieces in half again, how many biscuit pieces does she now have in total?

Answer: ....

Can you fill in the missing numbers in each of these number triangles, so that every square and circle contains a number? Each square should contain the result of multiplying the two circled numbers on either side of it.

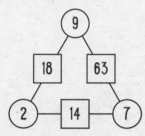

In this example,
2 x 9 = 18,
9 x 7 = 63 and
2 x 7 = 14.

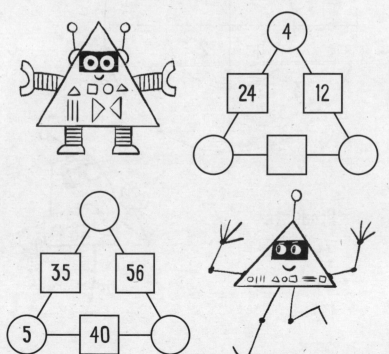

TIME ....

Can you form the products below by choosing one number from each ring on this dartboard and then multiplying them together?

For example, you could form a product of 14 by picking 2 from the inner ring and 7 from the outer ring.

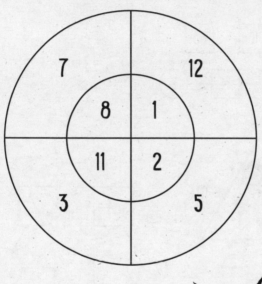

Products:

33 = ...

56 = ...

132 = ...

To solve this diagonal multiplication puzzle, place the numbers 1 to 3 once each into every row and column. Each of the numbers outside the grid tells you the product of the diagonal numbers pointed to by the arrow.

Here's an example to show you how the puzzle works:

In these diagonal lines, for instance, 3 x 3 = 9 and 1 x 3 = 3

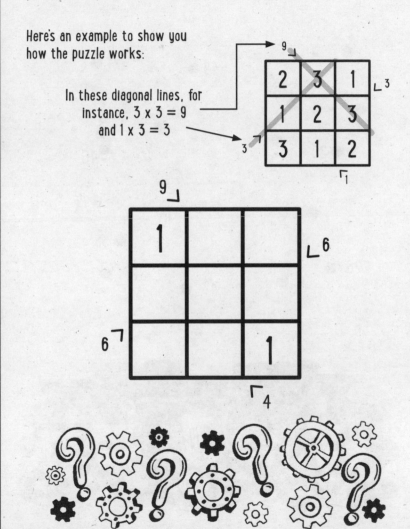

TIME ....

Complete this dot-to-dot puzzle by joining multiples of 5 in increasing numerical order to reveal something you'd find underwater. Ignore any numbers that are not multiples of 5.

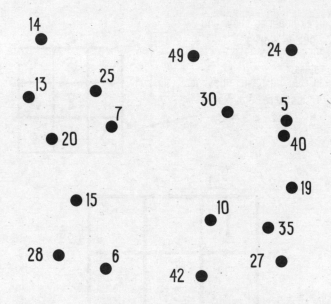

14

49   24

13   25   30   5

7   40

20

19

15   10   35

28   6   42   27

Three different digits, A, B and C, have been used to write down
two multiplication calculations from the times tables. Can you
work out the value of each digit? A digit is any number from 0 to
9 and they have the same value in both calculations.

For example, if you thought A = 5, B = 7 and C = 9, then the first
calculation would be read as 57 x 55 = 597 (which is incorrect).
No advanced mathematics is required – only the use of the 1 to 12
times tables.

$$AB \times AA = ACB$$
$$C \times 7 = BA$$

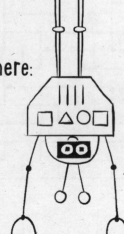

Write your answers here:

A = ...

B = ...

C = ...

Can you help this robo-pup find a route through the maze from START to FINISH? Multiply together all the numbers that your route must cross over. What is the resulting product?

The product is:

....

This robot is opening a sweetshop. He has worked out the area of two rooms in the shop. Can you use this information to calculate the area of the third room, indicated by the question mark?

All three rooms in the shop are squares. Remember that the area of a square is equal to its width times its height. This puzzle is designed to put your times-tables skills to the test in a new way, so don't worry if you find it tricky!

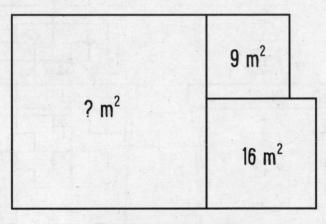

$? \text{ m}^2$

9 m^2

16 m^2

The third room is:

.... m²

These robots are professional smoothie makers. Can you work out how many pieces of fruit each one is putting in their blender by completing these calculations?

Begin with the number at the START of each sequence, then complete the calculations until you reach the end. Write your answer after the equals symbol. See if you can do all the maths in your head, without making any written notes.

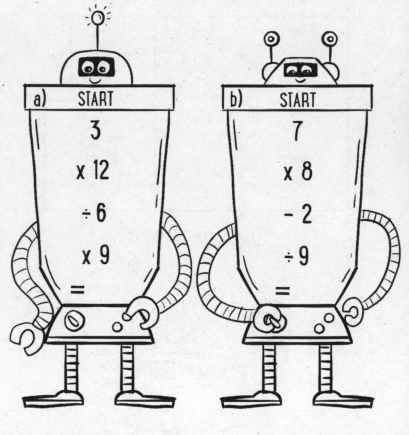

a) START
3
x 12
÷ 6
x 9
=

b) START
7
x 8
- 2
÷ 9
=

Look at these picture equations. Can you work out the value of each of the following robo-pets? No robo-pet has a value higher than 12.

 x = 30

 x = 12

 x = 10

Write your answers here:

 = ...

 = ...

 = ...

Can you solve these written multiplication puzzles?

a) Kanishka has three bananas. She carefully cuts each banana into three pieces, and then cuts each of those pieces into three more pieces. How many pieces of banana does she now have in total?

Answer: ....

b) A robot family has three children in it and the product of their three ages is 72. If the eldest child is double the age of the youngest child, then how old are each of the children?

Answer: ....

This next puzzle is designed to really put your knowledge of the 1 to 12 times tables to the test! The same digit is missing from all of the following numbers. If that digit was added back in then all the numbers would be products from the times tables. The numbers must come from the 1 to 12 times tables, from 1 x 1 to 12 x 12.

For example, if you had 14_ and _0 then the missing digit would be 4 because 144 and 40 are both products in the times tables (144 is the product of 12 x 12 and 40 is the product of 5 x 8 or 8 x 5 and 4 x 10 or 10 x 4).

Which digit is missing from the following times-tables products?

4_
_5
2_
_0
3_
1_

To solve these calcudoku puzzles, place the numbers 1 to 4 once each into every row and column. You must place these numbers so that the values in each bold-lined region of grid squares multiply to give the small number printed in the top left-hand corner of the region.

This finished puzzle shows you how it works:

For example, these two bold-lined areas each contain numbers that multiply to make 12 (4 x 3 x 1 and 4 x 3)

12 3	1	4	6 2
4	2 2	1	3
2 2	12 4	3	8 1
1	3	2	4

Puzzle 1

8			6
3	12	4	
2			1
	24		

Puzzle 2

48		2	
	1	6	
6		1	48
2			

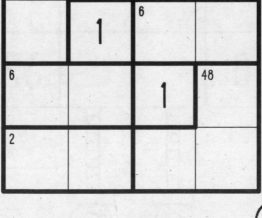

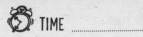

A section of the times-tables grid is displayed on this robot, but some of the values are missing. Can you work out what the sequences are and fill in all the numbers? If you need a reminder, you can always turn back to the grid in the introduction, but try to fill it in from memory first.

Can you place the numbers 4, 6, 7 and 8 once each into the empty squares so that all the mathematical calculations are correct? Two calculations read from left to right and two read from top to bottom.

This robot has bought a bunch of balloons and each one has a different number painted on it.

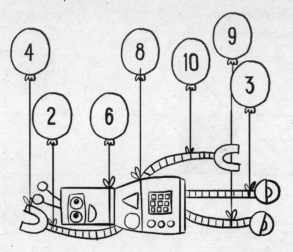

Can you work out which balloons you need to burst so that the remaining numbers multiply together to form the following totals? For example, you could form a total of 16 by bursting all the balloons except 2 and 8, since 2 x 8 = 16. You can leave more than two balloons to reach your answer.

Write your answers here:

a) 20 = ...

b) 27 = ...

c) 32 = ...

d) 64 = ...

Can you crack this frame sudoku puzzle? Place the numbers 3, 5, 7 or 9 once each into every row, column and bold-lined 2x2 box. The numbers outside the grid tell you the product of the nearest numbers in the corresponding row or column.

Here's an example:

For instance, 7 x 3 = 21 and 9 x 7 = 63

TIMES-TABLES GAME 49 →

Can you fill in the missing numbers in these multiplication sequences? Each sequence is made up of two overlapping times tables. The first sequence contains both the 2 times table and the 5 times table, and has been completed to show you how it works. Remember that the sequences go up in increasing numerical order, so they don't always alternate between times tables.

For example:

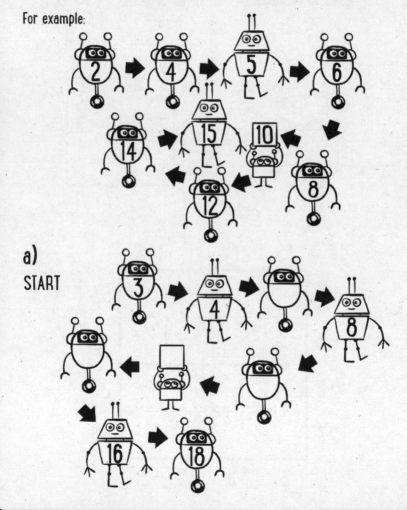

a)
START

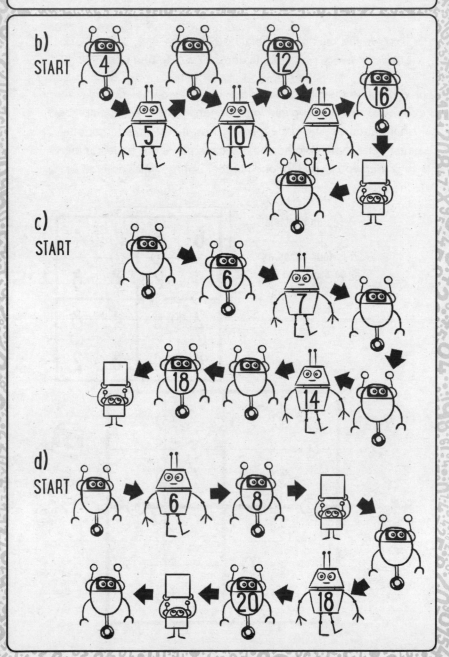

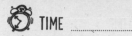

To solve the 'multiples' sudoku below, place 2, 4, 6 and 8 once each into every row, column and 2x2 bold-lined box.

When two touching squares are joined by a small circled number, it shows that there's a multiple connection between the numbers in the squares. The circle tells you how many times larger one number is than the other. So, for example, if the circle contains a 3 then you know that one number is three times as large as the other.

Here's an example:

8 is four times as large as 2, and 6 is three times as large as 2

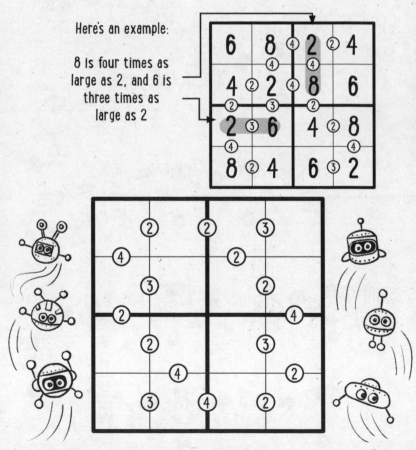

Complete each of these multiplication calculations and then find them hidden in the grid below. The calculations can be written in any direction, including diagonally, and may read either forwards or backwards (don't get confused by the backwards ones!). One is solved for you already as an example: 4 × 7 = 28

4 × 7 = 28   _ × 4 = 16   6 × 7 = __

2 × _ = 6   4 × 8 = __   _ × 2 = 14

2 × _ = 10   _ × 4 = 20   8 × 6 = __

2 × _ = 16   5 × _ = 40   _ × _ = 56

3 × _ = 15   6 × 2 = __   8 × 8 = __

3 × _ = 24

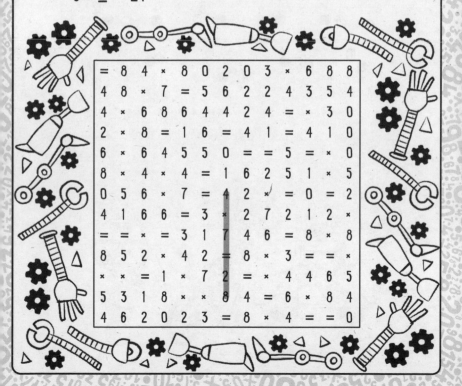

=	8	4	×	8	0	2	0	3	×	6	8	8
4	8	×	7	=	5	6	2	2	4	3	5	4
4	×	6	8	6	4	4	2	4	=	×	3	0
2	×	8	=	1	6	=	4	1	=	4	1	0
6	×	6	4	5	5	0	=	=	5	=	×	0
8	×	4	=	4	=	1	6	2	5	1	×	5
0	5	6	×	7	=	4	2	×	=	0	=	2
4	1	6	6	=	3	×	2	7	2	1	2	×
=	=	×	=	3	1	7	4	6	=	8	×	8
8	5	2	×	4	2	=	8	×	3	=	=	×
×	×	=	1	×	7	2	=	4	4	6	5	
5	3	1	8	×	×	8	4	=	6	×	8	4
4	6	2	0	2	3	=	8	×	4	=	=	0

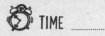

Complete this dot-to-dot puzzle by joining multiples of 4 in increasing numerical order to reveal a hidden method of transport. Ignore any numbers that are not multiples of 4.

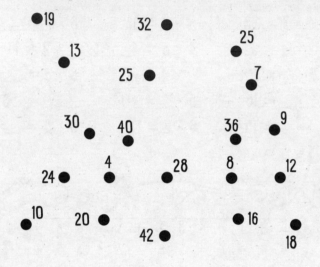

●19   32 ●

  13 ●   25 ●

     25 ●   7 ●

30 ●   40 ●   36 ●   9 ●

  4 ●   28 ●   8 ●   12 ●

24 ●

10 ●   20 ●   ● 16

      42 ●   18 ●

To solve this diagonal multiplication puzzle, place the numbers 2, 3 or 5 once each into every row and column. The numbers outside the grid tell you the product of the diagonal numbers pointed to by the arrow.

Here's an example to show you how it works:

For instance, 2 x 3 = 6 and 2 x 2 = 4

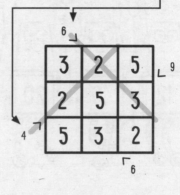

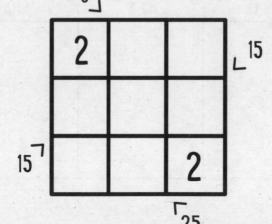

Can you place each of the following numbers into the columns below, so that every column contains two numbers? Be careful, as some of the numbers will fit into more than one column but there is only one way of fitting two numbers into each column.

TWO MULTIPLES OF 4	TWO MULTIPLES OF 6	TWO MULTIPLES OF 8

Can you form the products below by choosing one number from each ring on this dartboard and then multiplying them together?

For example, you could make 30 by picking 5 from the innermost ring, 1 from the middle ring and 6 from the outermost ring.

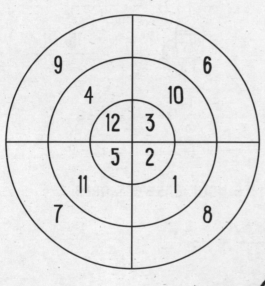

Products:

48 = ...

64 = ...

132 = ...

Look at these picture equations. Can you work out the value of each of the following mini-bots? All of the mini-bots have different values and no mini-bot has a value higher than 12.

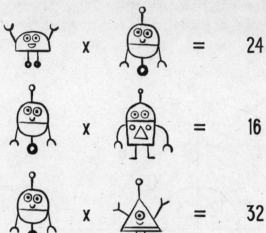

Write your answers here:

Can you draw lines to join the numbers in the first, second and third columns to create five correct multiplications? One has already been done to show you how the puzzle works, since 6 x 5 = 30. Be careful, as there is more than one way to create some products but there is only one way of using every robot exactly once each.

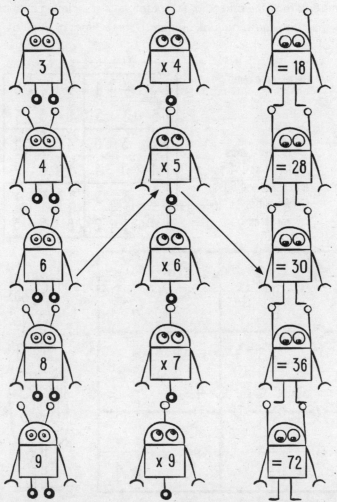

To solve the 'multiples' sudoku below, place 1 to 6 once each into every row, column and 3x2 bold-lined box.

When two touching squares are joined by a small circled number, it shows that there's a multiple connection between the numbers in the squares. The circle tells you how many times larger one number is than the other. So, for example, if the circle contains a 3 then you know that one number is three times as large as the other.

Here's an example:

5 is five times as large as 1, for instance, and 6 is two times as large as 3

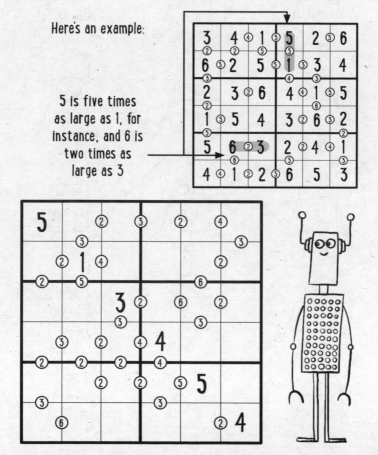

A section of the times-tables grid is displayed on this robot, but some of the values are missing. Can you work out what the sequences are and fill in all the numbers? If you need a reminder, you can always turn back to the grid in the introduction, but try to fill it in from memory first.

Can you fill in the missing numbers in each of these number triangles, so that every square and circle contains a number? Each square should contain the result of multiplying the two circled numbers on either side of it.

In this example,
2 x 9 = 18,
9 x 7 = 63 and
2 x 7 = 14

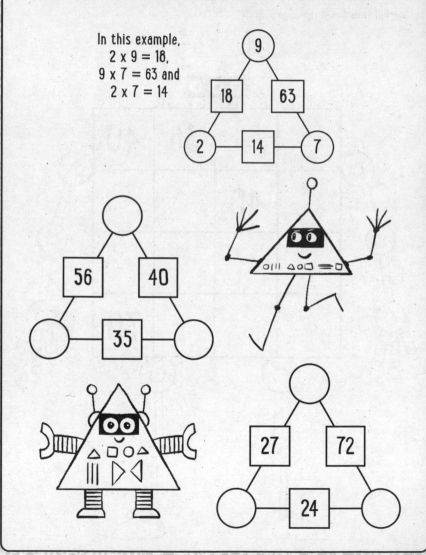

Can you place the numbers 1 to 8 once each into the empty squares so that all the multiplication calculations are correct? Three calculations read from left to right and three read from top to bottom. One number is already placed, to help you get started.

TIMES-TABLES GAME 62 ⟶

Can you crack the 'killer sudoku' puzzles on the opposite page?
You need to place the numbers 1 to 4 once each into every row,
column and bold-lined 2x2 box. Each dashed-line region also
has a number printed in its top left-hand corner. To complete the
puzzle correctly, all of the numbers that you place in that region
must multiply together to give that value.

Have a look at this example
to see how it works:

In this dashed-line region,
for instance,
1 x 4 x 2 = 8

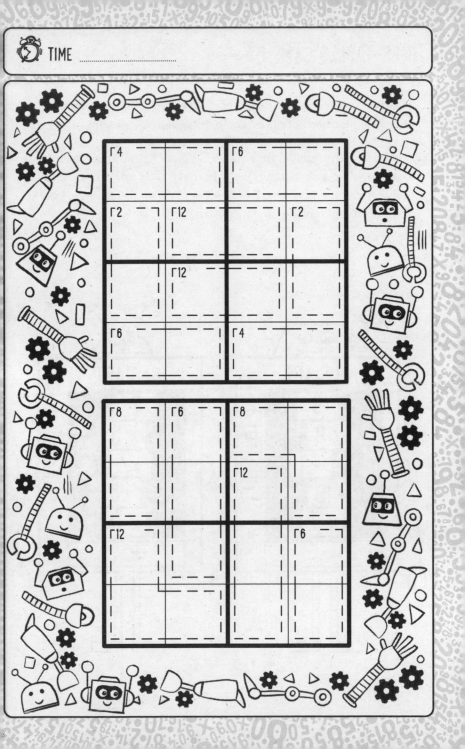

Can you work out how many snacks are available from these vending machine robots by completing the calculations?

Begin with the number at the START of each sequence, then complete the calculations until you reach the end. Write your answer in the empty box. See if you can do all the maths in your head, without making any written notes.

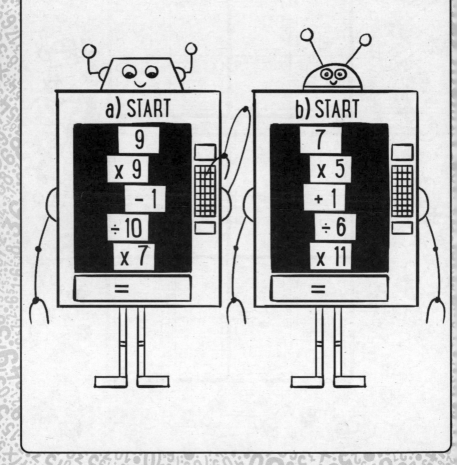

Can you conquer these number pyramids? Write a number in each empty box so that every block contains a number equal to the product of the two numbers directly beneath it.

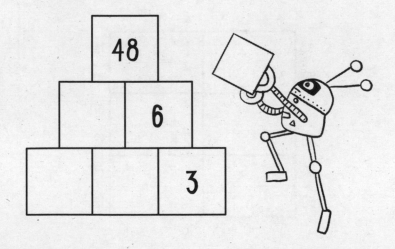

To solve this frame sudoku puzzle, place 1 to 6 once each into every row, column and bold-lined 3x2 box. The numbers outside the grid tell you the product of the nearest numbers in the corresponding row or column, reading up to the first bold line.

Here's how it works:

For instance, 6 x 2 = 12 and 1 x 6 x 5 = 30

	15	4	12	15	12	4	
10	5	1	2	3	6	4	72
72	3	4	6	5	2	1	10
30	1	6	5	2	4	3	24
24	4	2	3	6	1	5	30
30	6	5	1	4	3	2	24
24	2	3	4	1	5	6	30
	12	15	4	4	15	12	

	6	4	30	4	10	18	
48				1	5	3	15
15	3						48
12			2				60
60				2			12
12						5	60
60		5					12
	24	10	3	18	4	10	

In each of the following calculations, there is one extra digit that shouldn't be there. Can you cross it out so that each calculation is correct?

For example, 12 x 4 = 8 can be fixed by crossing out 1 to leave 2 x 4 = 8.

a) 7 x 12 x 6 = 42

b) 10 x 11 x 12 = 120

c) 3 x 67 x 2 = 36

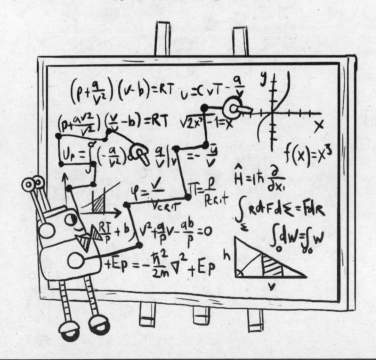

Can you fill in the missing numbers in these multiplication sequences? Each sequence is made up of two overlapping times tables. The first sequence contains both the 2 times table and the 5 times table, and has been completed to show you how it works. Remember that the sequences go up in increasing numerical order, so they don't always alternate between times tables.

For example:

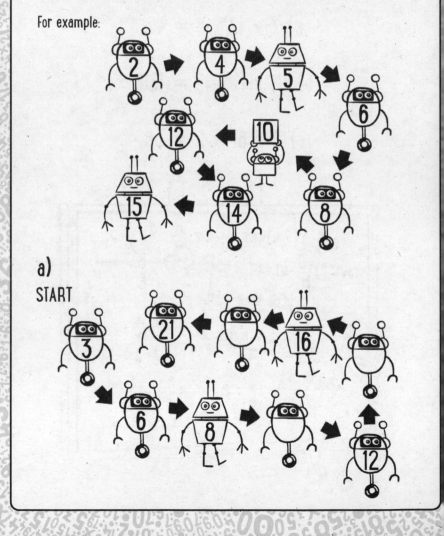

a)
START

b)
START

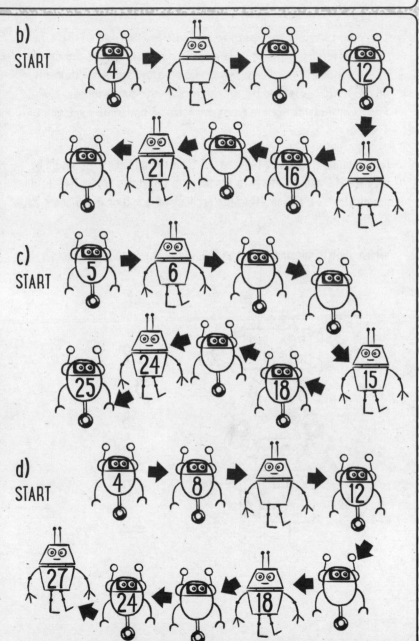

c)
START

d)
START

This next puzzle is designed to put your knowledge of the 1 to 12 times tables to the test! The same digit is missing from all of the following numbers. If that digit was added back in then all the numbers would be products from the times tables. The numbers must come from the 1 to 12 times tables, from 1 x 1 up to 12 x 12.

For example, if you had 14_ and _0 then the missing digit would be 4, because 144 and 40 are both products in the times tables (144 is the product of 12 x 12 and 40 is the product of 5 x 8 or 8 x 5 and 4 x 10 or 10 x 4).

Which digit is missing from the following times-tables products?

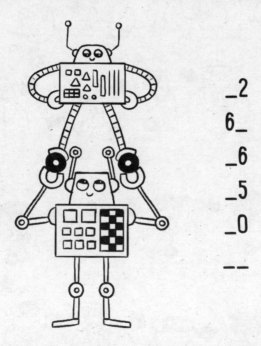

_2

6_

_6

_5

_0

--

Can you solve these written multiplication puzzles?

a) Pedro has some bottles of juice for sale on his market stall. The bottles arrived in boxes, but unfortunately three bottles in each box were broken, so he has thrown these away rather than put them out for sale. He started off with five boxes of apple juice and five boxes of orange juice, and each box had ten bottles in it, including the broken ones. Given that he has put out all of the unbroken bottles, how many bottles does he now have out for sale?

Answer: ....

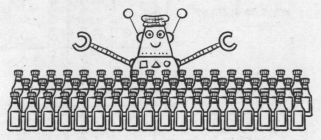

b) Three children under 12 are waiting to have their photograph taken at a local studio. One of the children is greater in age than the sum of the other two children's ages. No two children have the same age. When you multiply all three children's ages together the product is 99. How old is each of the children?

Answer: ....

TIME ....

To solve the 'multiples' sudoku below, place the numbers 1, 2, 3, 7, 8 or 9 once each into every row, column and 3x2 bold-lined box.

When two touching squares are joined by a small circled number, it shows that there's a multiple connection between the numbers in the squares. The circle tells you how many times larger one number is than the other. So, for example, if the circle contains a 3 then you know that one number is three times as large as the other.

Here's an example:

For instance, 8 is four times as large as 2 and 9 is nine times as large as 1

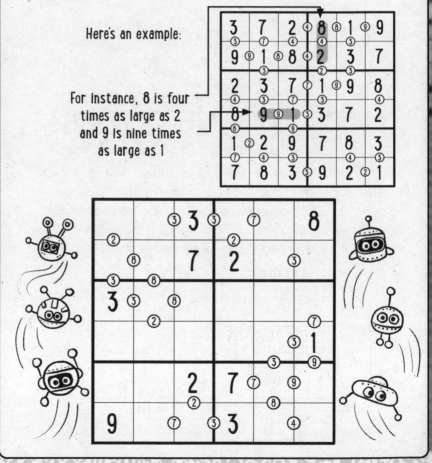

Help this robot complete his artwork. Colour in the shapes in the puzzle below according to the following rules, to reveal a hidden picture.

Multiples of:

3 = blue
4 = red
5 = purple
7 = orange
11 = black

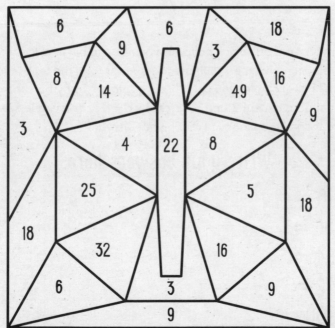

This robot has bought a bunch of balloons and each one has a different number painted on it.

Can you work out which balloons you need to burst so that the remaining numbers multiply together to form the following totals? For example, you could form a total of 16 by bursting all the balloons except 2 and 8, since 2 x 8 = 16. You can leave more than two balloons to reach your answer.

Write your answers here:

a) 18 = ...

b) 36 = ...

c) 64 = ...

d) 72 = ...

e) 100 = ...

Complete this dot-to-dot puzzle by joining multiples of 8 in increasing numerical order to reveal a spooky creature. Ignore any numbers that are not multiples of 8.

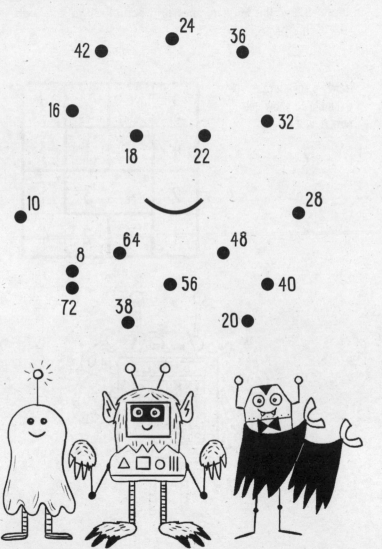

24
36
42
16
32
18   22
10
28
64   48
8
56   40
72
38
20

To solve these calcudoku puzzles, place the numbers 1 to 4 once each into every row and column. You must place these numbers so that the values in each bold-lined region of grid squares multiply to give the small number printed in the top left-hand corner of the region.

Here's a completed example to show you how it works:

12 3	1	4	6 2
4	2 2	1	3
2 2	12 4	3	8 1
1	3	2	4

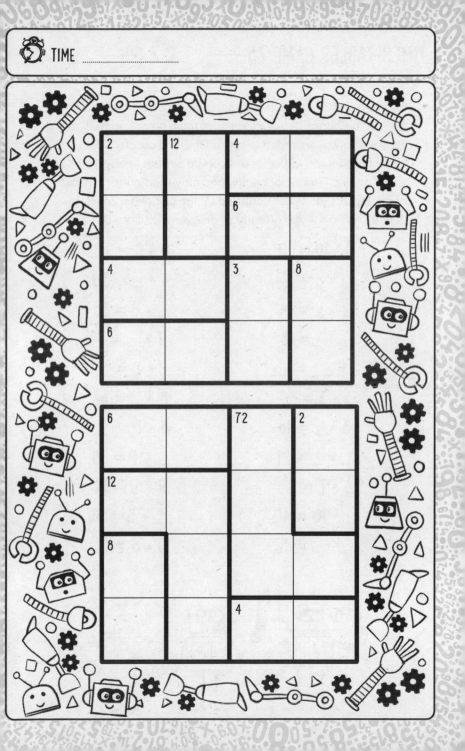

Puzzle 1

2	12	4	
		6	
4		3	8
6			

Puzzle 2

6		72	2
12			
8			
		4	

Can you find all of these multiplication calculations in the grid on the opposite page? Some of them have two missing numbers so you will need to search the grid carefully for possible solutions. Calculations can be written in any direction, including diagonally, and may read either forwards or backwards (don't get confused by the backwards ones!). One is solved for you already as an example: 1 × 10 = 10

1 × 10 = 10   5 × 8 = __

1 × 6 = _   6 × _ = 30

2 × _ = 14   _ × 6 = 36

_ × _= 18   7 × _ = 7

2 × __ = __   _ × 7 = __

3 × 5 = __   8 × _ = 32

3 × _ = 18   8 × 7 = __

_ × _ = 21   _ × 4 = 36

4 × 7 = __   9 × _ = 81

_ × 10 = 40   __ × 3 = 30

_ × _ = 5   10 × 8 = 8_

1	8	=	9	×	9	9	×	4	=	3	6	3
6	5	=	7	×	8	2	5	6	4	6	×	1
4	=	5	0	1	2	×	×	=	7	8	8	1
×	5	×	8	9	×	1	8	6	4	×	1	2
=	=	1	=	4	7	0	=	×	=	1	=	=
×	×	=	8	=	=	=	4	1	4	0	6	7
4	8	5	×	7	1	2	0	1	4	=	×	×
×	1	1	0	×	4	0	0	=	1	2	3	3
7	=	=	1	7	=	×	0	6	7	1	8	2
=	9	5	=	3	3	1	6	×	6	=	3	6
2	×	×	=	=	×	0	1	=	0	1	×	1
8	2	3	3	4	9	0	3	=	5	×	6	0
1	5	0	4	3	7	=	1	×	7	1	×	×

Look at these picture equations. Can you work out the value of each of the following droids? No droid has a value higher than 12.

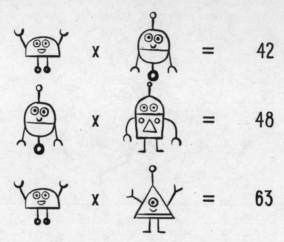

Write your answers here:

A section of the times-tables grid is displayed on this robot, but some of the values are missing. Can you work out what the sequences are and fill in all the numbers? If you need a reminder, you can always turn back to the grid in the introduction, but try to fill it in from memory first.

To solve this diagonal multiplication puzzle, place the numbers 1 to 4 once each into every row and column. Each of the numbers outside the grid tell you the product of the diagonal numbers pointed to by the arrow.

Here's a finished puzzle to show you how it works:

For instance, 2 x 1 x 4 = 8 and 3 x 2 = 6

	8↓	6↓		
	4	2	3	1	⌐4
	3	4	1	2	⌐16
6	1	3	2	4	
12⌐	2	1	4	3	
		⌐1	⌐36		

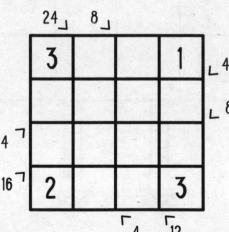

	24↓	8↓			
	3			1	⌐4
					⌐8
4⌐					
16⌐	2			3	
		⌐4	⌐12		

Can you place each of the following numbers into the columns below, so that every column contains two numbers? Be careful, as some numbers will fit into more than one column but there is only one way of fitting two numbers into each column.

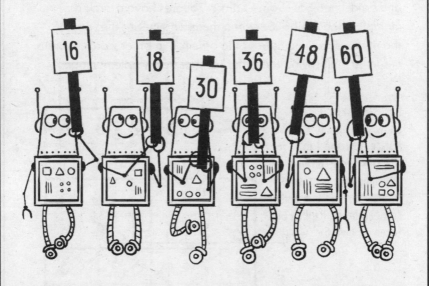

TWO MULTIPLES OF 6	TWO MULTIPLES OF 8	TWO MULTIPLES OF 12

Can you help this scientist robot fix his inventing machine? To reboot the machine, you need to solve the 'multiples' sudoku on the opposite page.

Place the numbers 1 to 6 once each into every row, column and bold-lined box. Some pairs of squares have a circled multiplication symbol between them. This means that one of the numbers is a multiple of the other or, in other words, can be made by multiplying the other number by a whole number.

Here's an example to show you how it works. Notice how the 1 in the first row can be multiplied by four to give 4, and the 2 in the third row can be multiplied by three to give 6.

1	4	5	2	3	6
3	6	2	4	5	1
4	1	6	3	2	5
2	5	3	1	6	4
6	2	4	5	1	3
5	3	1	6	4	2

Help this robot find the shortest possible route through the maze, from START at the top to FINISH at the bottom. Multiply together all the numbers that your route crosses over. What is the resulting product?

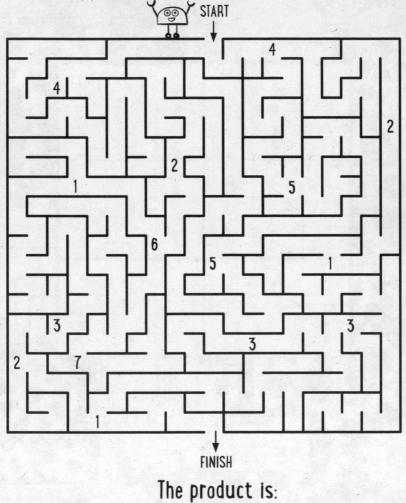

START

4

4

2

2

1

5

6

5

1

3

3

2   7   3

1

FINISH

The product is:

....

Can you fill in the missing numbers in each of these number triangles, so that every square and circle contains a number? Each square should contain the result of multiplying the two circled numbers on either side of it.

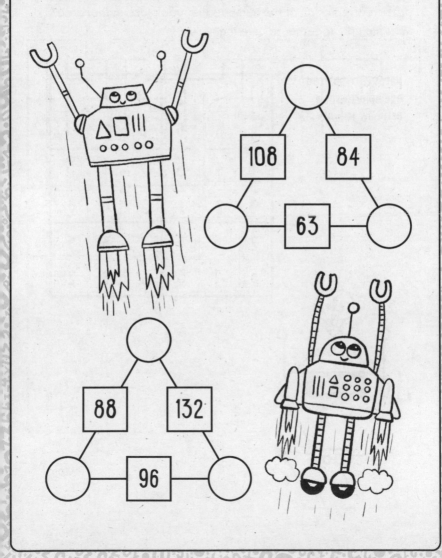

Can you crack the 'killer sudoku' puzzle on the opposite page? You need to place the numbers 1 to 6 once each into every row, column and bold-lined 3x2 box. Each dashed-line region also has a number printed in its top left-hand corner. To complete the puzzle correctly, all of the numbers that you place in that area must multiply together to give that value.

Here's a completed example to show you how it works:

3		60	90		4
1	3	2	6	5	4
20				6	
4	5	6	3	2	1
24			40		
6	4	5	2	1	3
36				24	
3	2	1	5	4	6
10		12		15	
2	6	4	1	3	5
5	1	3	4	6	2

30		2		24	36
					4
24		20			
	1				
2		30	6		
			3		
20	36			40	
		6			**4**
		12		**2**	
	2	6		15	

TIMES-TABLES GAME 84 → ⏰ TIME ....

Can you form the products below by choosing one number from each ring of this dartboard and then multiplying them together?

For example, you could form a product of 28 by picking 7 from the innermost ring, 2 from the middle ring and 2 from the outermost ring.

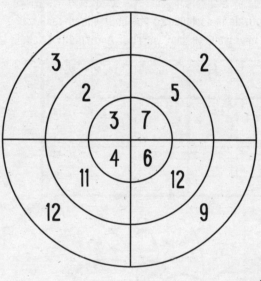

Products:

12 = ...

40 = ...

54 = ...

These two robots are trying to work out the area of the shapes below. The area of the overall rectangle shown below is 88 cm². Each of the dotted shapes inside it is a perfect square, and both grey rectangles have the same height. What is the area of each dotted square?

Remember that the area of a shape or rectangle is equal to its width times its height. This puzzle is designed to put your times-tables skills to the test in a new way, so don't worry if you find it tricky!

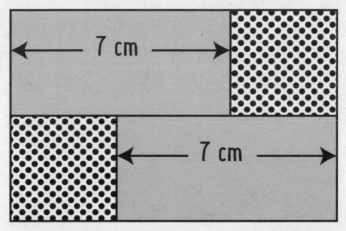

← 7 cm →

7 cm →

The dotted squares each have an area of:
.... cm²

Can you conquer this number pyramid challenge? Write a number in each empty block, so that every block contains a number equal to the product of the two numbers directly beneath it.

Take a look at this completed example to see how it works:

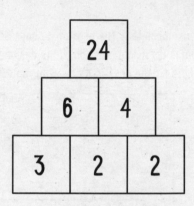

24

6 | 4

3 | 2 | 2

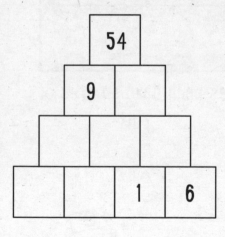

54

9

1 | 6

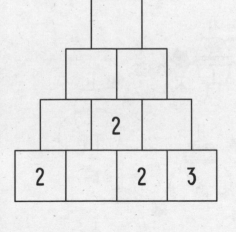

TIMES-TABLES GAME 87 ⟶

Can you fill in the missing numbers in these multiplication sequences? Each sequence is made up of two overlapping times tables. The first sequence contains both the 2 times table and the 5 times table, and has been completed to show you how it works. Remember that the sequences go up in increasing numerical order, so they don't always alternate between times tables.

For example:

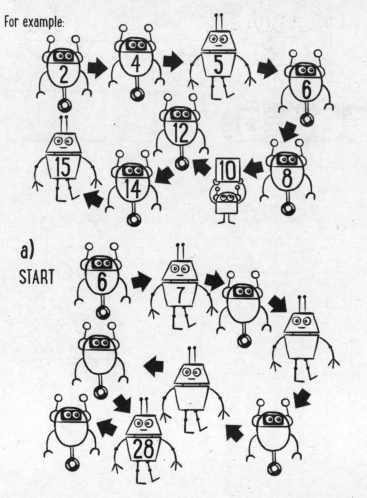

a)
START

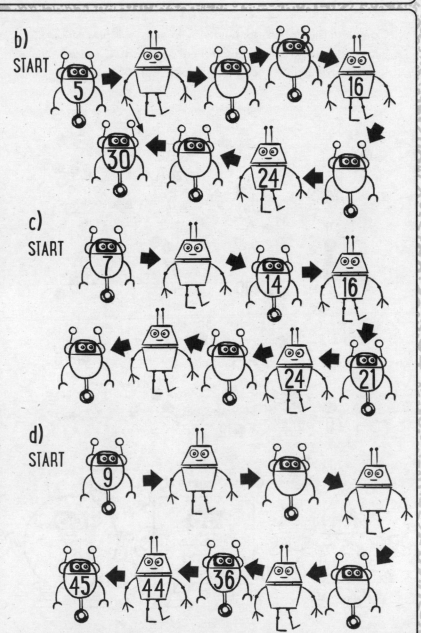

b) START 5 16 30 24

c) START 7 14 16 24 21

d) START 9 45 44 36

TIMES-TABLES GAME 88 →

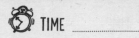 TIME ....

Complete this dot-to-dot puzzle by joining multiples of 7 in increasing numerical order to reveal a hidden 3D shape. Ignore any numbers that are not multiples of 7.

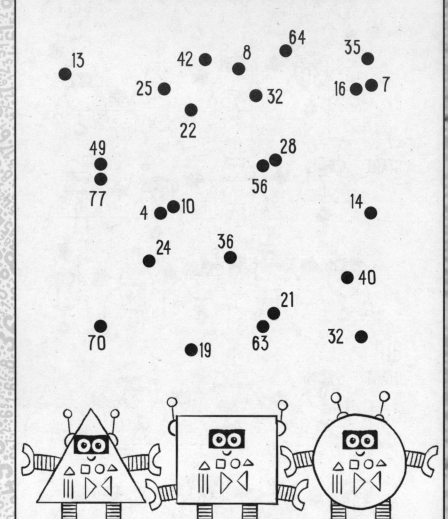

Can you draw lines to join the numbers in the first, second and third columns to create five correct multiplications? One has already been done to show you how the puzzle works, since 7 x 5 = 35. Be careful, as there is more than one way to create some products but there is only one way of using every robot exactly once each.

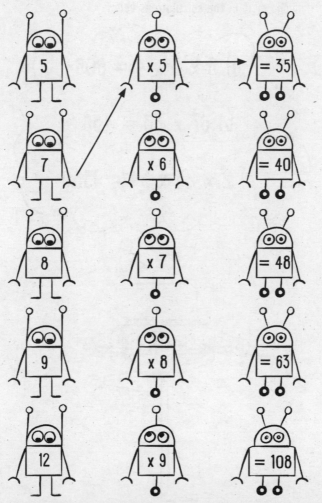

In each of the following calculations, there is at least one extra digit that shouldn't be there. Can you cross the wrong digits out so that each calculation is correct?

For example, 12 x 100 = 1230 can be fixed by crossing out a 0 in 100 and the 3 in 1230 to leave 12 x 10 = 120. You may need to cross out more than one digit in the calculations below.

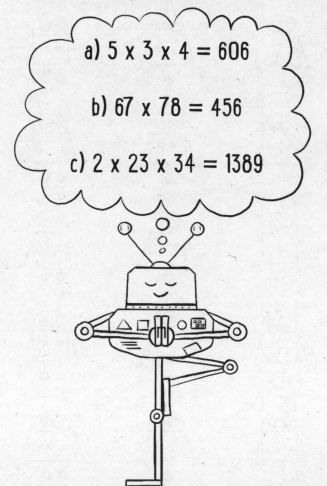

a) 5 x 3 x 4 = 606

b) 67 x 78 = 456

c) 2 x 23 x 34 = 1389

This next puzzle is designed to put your knowledge of the 1 to 12 times tables to the test! The same digit is missing from all of the following numbers. If that digit was added back in then all the numbers would be products from the times tables. The numbers must come from the 1 to 12 times tables, from 1 x 1 to 12 x 12.

For example, if you had 14_ and _0 then the missing digit would be 4, because 144 and 40 are both products in the times tables (144 is the product of 12 x 12 and 40 is the product of 5 x 8 or 8 x 5 and 4 x 10 or 10 x 4).

Which digit is missing from the following times-tables products?

3_

_4

1_

_0

9_

5_

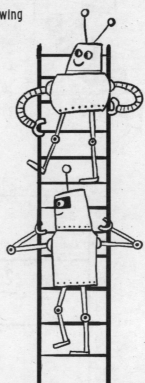

Can you crack this frame sudoku puzzle? Place the numbers 1 to 6 once each into every row, column and bold-lined 3x2 box. The numbers outside the grid tell you the product of the nearest numbers in the corresponding row or column, reading up to the first bold line.

For instance, 6 x 2 = 12 and 1 x 6 x 5 = 30

Here's an example:

Example grid:

	15	4	12	15	12	4	
10	5	1	2	3	6	4	72
72	3	4	6	5	2	1	10
30	1	6	5	2	4	3	24
24	4	2	3	6	1	5	30
30	6	5	1	4	3	2	24
24	2	3	4	1	5	6	30
	12	15	4	4	15	12	

Puzzle grid:

	10	3	24	30	2	12	
36	2						20
20							36
30			2				24
24				3			30
36							20
20						6	36
	6	8	15	2	12	30	

This robot has bought a bunch of balloons, and each one has a different number painted on it.

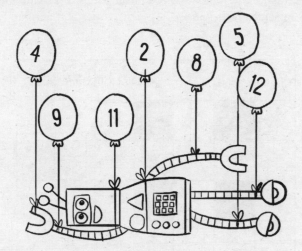

Can you work out which balloons you need to burst so that the remaining numbers multiply together to form each of the following totals? For example, you could form a total of 16 by bursting all balloons except 2 and 8, since 2 x 8 = 16. You can leave more than 2 balloons to reach your answer.

Write your answers here:

a) 24 = ...

b) 64 = ...

c) 80 = ...

d) 132 = ...

Can you place the numbers 1 to 6 and 8 to 9 once each into the empty squares so that each of the multiplication calculations is correct? Three calculations read from left to right and three read from top to bottom.

A section of the times-tables grid is displayed on this robot, but some of the values are missing. Can you work out what the sequences are and fill in all the numbers? If you need a reminder, you can always turn back to the grid in the introduction, but try to fill it in from memory first.

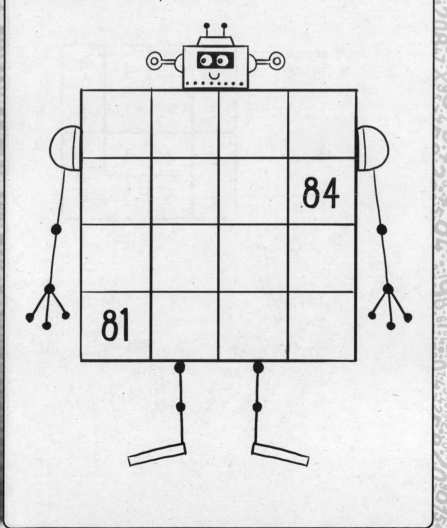

To solve the calcudoku puzzles on the opposite page, place the numbers 1 to 4 once each into every row and column. You must place these numbers so that the values in each bold-lined region of grid squares multiply to give the small number printed in the top left-hand corner of the region.

Here's an example to show you how it works:

12			6
3	1	4	2
4	2	1	3
2	12		8
2	4	3	1
1	3	2	4

Puzzle 1

24			6
4			
8		12	
	6		

Puzzle 2

72			6
8			4
	2	12	

Look at these picture equations. Can you work out the value of each of the following robo-fish? No robo-fish has a value higher than 12.

[fish] x [fish] x [fish] = 84

[fish] x [fish] = 15

[fish] x [fish] = 35

Write your answers here:

[fish] = ...

[fish] = ...

[fish] = ...

[fish] = ...

These robots have spent weeks growing two sunflower plants. Can you work out how many times each robot has watered their plant by completing the calculations below?

Begin with the number at the START of each calculation, then complete the sums in the sequence, going up the plant until you reach the flower. Write your answer in the empty box at the top of the flower. See if you can do all the maths in your head, without making any written notes.

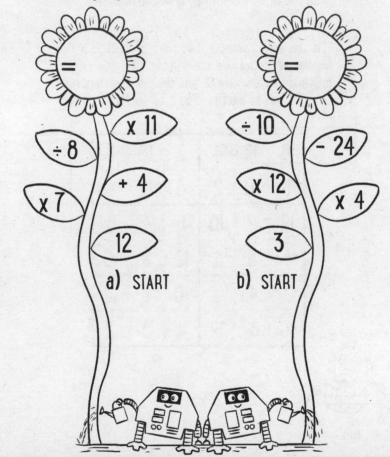

This robot inventor is locked out of his lab. To open the door, he needs to complete the 'multiples' sudoku puzzle on the opposite page.

Place 2, 4, 6, 8, 10 or 12 once each into every row, column and bold-lined box. Some pairs of squares have a circled multiplication symbol between them. This means that one of the numbers is a multiple of the other or, in other words, can be made by multiplying the other number by a whole number.

In this solved example, two pairs of squares are highlighted. Notice how the 4 in the first row can be multiplied by 3 to give 12, and the 6 in the third row can be multiplied by 2 to give 12.

8	12	4	2	10	6
6	10	2	8	12	4
12	2	10	6	4	8
4	8	6	12	2	10
2	4	8	10	6	12
10	6	12	4	8	2

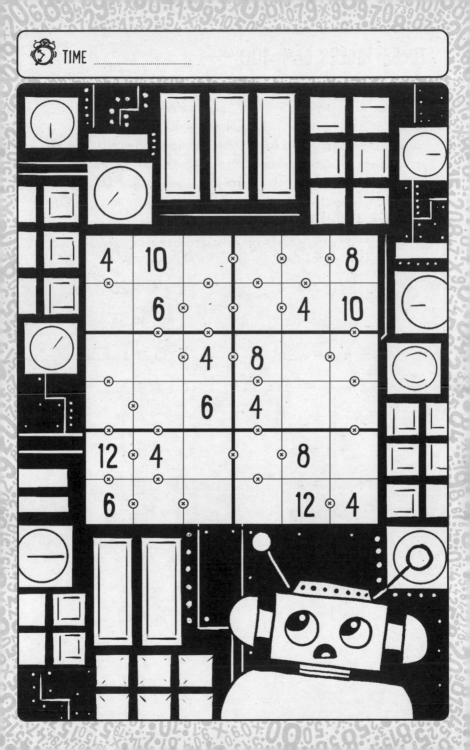

TIMES-TABLES GAME 100 →

Can you find all of these multiplication calculations in the grid? Some of them have two missing numbers, so you will need to search the grid carefully for possible solutions. The calculations can be written in any direction, including diagonally, and may read either forwards or backwards (don't get confused by the backwards ones!). One is solved for you already as an example: $11 \times 11 = 121$

$11 \times 11 = 121$ $6 \times \_\_ = 72$

$1 \times \_ = 7$ $\_ \times 4 = 28$

$\_ \times 3 = 6$ $7 \times \_ = 63$

$2 \times \_ = \_\_$ $8 \times 3 = \_\_$

$2 \times \_\_ = 24$ $8 \times 7 = \_\_$

$3 \times 5 = \_\_$ $\_ \times 2 = 18$

$\_ \times 4 = 16$ $9 \times \_ = 81$

$4 \times \_ = 36$ $10 \times \_ = 10$

$\_ \times 11 = 44$ $\_\_ \times 11 = 110$

$5 \times \_ = 35$ $\_\_ \times \_ = 66$

$6 \times \_ = 24$ $12 \times \_ = 72$

$\_ \times 9 = \_\_$ $12 \times 12 = \_\_\_$

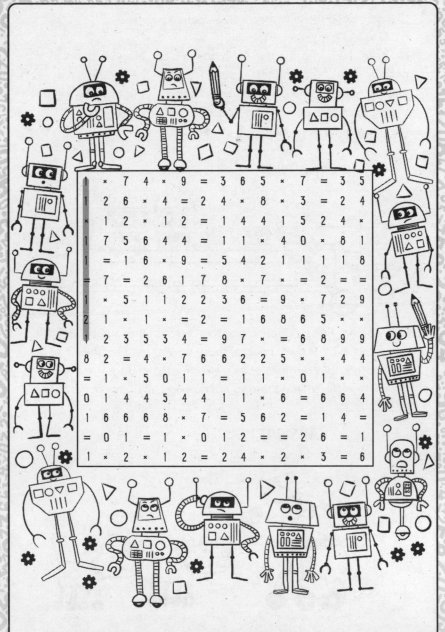

Can you solve these written multiplication puzzles?

a) Three children are going for a ride in a car, along with their parents. The oldest child is 1 year older than the middle child and the middle child is 1 year older than the youngest child. If the product of their ages is at least 25, but no more than 100, then how old is each of the children?

Answer:

b) A dog has three puppies, and then each of those puppies has two puppies of its own. Each of those newest puppies then also has another four puppies of its own. How many dogs are there now in total, including the original dog and all of the generations of puppies?

Answer:

All
of the
ANSWERS

TIMES-TABLES GAME 1

a) 2 x 3 x 2 x 5 = 60

b) 1 x 2 x 4 x 8 = 64

TIMES-TABLES GAME 2

$4 \times 5 = 20$ $3 \times 4 = 12$

$1 \times 4 = 4$ $3 \times 5 = 15$

$1 \times 5 = 5$ $4 \times 4 = 16$

$2 \times 5 = 10$ $5 \times 3 = 15$

$3 \times 2 = 6$ $5 \times 5 = 25$

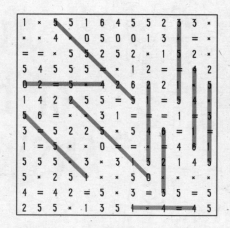

TIMES-TABLES GAME 3

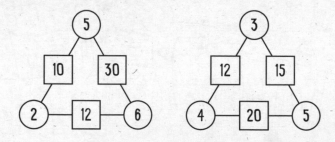

TIMES-TABLES GAME 4

🪛 = 2

🔧 = 4

🔩 = 5

TIMES-TABLES GAME 5

TIMES-TABLES GAME 6

a) Burst 6, 2 and 8 to leave $5 \times 3 = 15$

b) Burst 6, 5 and 2 to leave $3 \times 8 = 24$

c) Burst 5 and 8 to leave $2 \times 3 \times 6 = 36$

d) Burst 8 and 3 to leave $2 \times 5 \times 6 = 60$

TIMES-TABLES GAME 7

a) 2 times table: 2 4 6 8 10 12 14 16

b) 3 times table: 3 6 9 12 15 18 21 24

c) 6 times table: 6 12 18 24 30 36 42 48

d) 5 times table: 5 10 15 20 25 30 35 40

TIMES-TABLES GAME 8

4	×	2	=	8
×	■	×		
6	×	3	=	18
=		=		
24		6		

TIMES-TABLES GAME 9

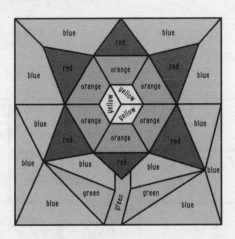

TIMES-TABLES GAME 10

The digit is '8', to give 81, 48, 28, 18, 88 and 84. One way to form these results in turn is from 9 x 9, 6 x 8, 4 x 7, 2 x 9, 8 x 11 and 7 x 12.

TIMES-TABLES GAME 11

4	6	8	10
6	9	12	15
8	12	16	20
10	15	20	25

TIMES-TABLES GAME 12

²1	2	3
⁶3	1	2
2	³3	1

²2	1	⁶3
³1	3	2
3	²2	1

TIMES-TABLES GAME 13

The route followed numbers in the 5 times table.

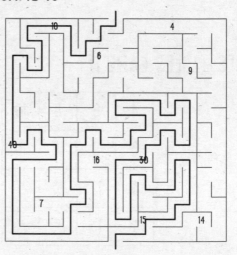

TIMES-TABLES GAME 14

20 = 2 x 10

40 = 4 x 10

84 = 12 x 7

TIMES-TABLES GAME 15

	12	2	3	8	
6	3	2	1	4	4
4	4	1	3	2	6
6	2	3	4	1	4
4	1	4	2	3	6
	2	12	8	3	

TIMES-TABLES GAME 16

Two Multiples of 3	Two Multiples of 4	Two Multiples of 6
15	16	18
21	36	30

TIMES-TABLES GAME 17

a) Tina had three, then had six. She gives away two, so now has four hats left.

b) The children are two and eight years old.

TIMES-TABLES GAME 18

A star

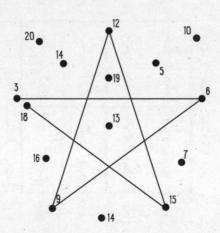

TIMES-TABLES GAME 19

a) 4 x 2 x 3 – 20 x 4 = 16

b) 5 x 2 x 10 – 95 x 7 = 35

c) 6 x 3 – 10 x 10 – 20 = 60

TIMES-TABLES GAME 20

2 x 5 = 10

3 x 3 = 9

4 x 6 = 24

6 x 2 = 12 (example)

7 x 4 = 28

TIMES-TABLES GAME 21

A = 1, B = 2, C = 0,
giving 12 x 10 = 120
and 11 x 11 = 121.

TIMES-TABLES GAME 22

= 3   = 4   = 6

TIMES-TABLES GAME 23

a) 7 x 3 = 21

b) 12 x 5 = 60

c) 1 x 11 x 12 = 132

TIMES-TABLES GAME 24

The reserved land has an area of 4 m², so it must be of dimensions
2 m x 2 m. This means that the length of each side of the garden
must be 2 m (as given with arrows to the side) + 2 m = 4 m.
In turn, its area is therefore 4 m x 4 m = **16 m²**.

TIMES-TABLES GAME 25

16	20	24	28
20	25	30	35
24	30	36	42
28	35	42	49

TIMES-TABLES GAME 26

a) 7 times table: 7 14 21 28 35 42 49 56

b) 4 times table: 4 8 12 16 20 24 28 32

c) 9 times table: 9 18 27 36 45 54 63 72

d) 10 times table: 10 20 30 40 50 60 70 80

TIMES-TABLES GAME 27

3	8	6	
1	4	2	3
3	2	4	1
4		3	8
4	1	3	2
6			
2	3	1	4

8		3	
2	4	1	3
	12	24	
1	3	2	4
			8
4	1	3	2
6			
3	2	4	1

TIMES-TABLES GAME 28

3 ③ 1	④ 4 ② 2
④	④
2 ② 4	④ 1 ③ 3
② ②	③
1 ② 2	3 4
④	④
4 3	2 ② 1

TIMES-TABLES GAME 29

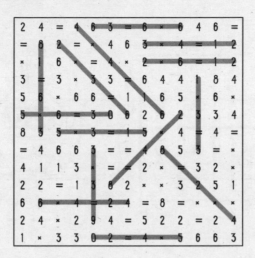

5 × 4 = 20	2 × 3 = 6	4 × 2 = 8	5 × 6 = 30
1 × 3 = 3	3 × 3 = 9	4 × 4 = 16	6 × 4 = 24
2 × 4 = 8	3 × 4 = 12	5 × 3 = 15	6 × 6 = 36
2 × 6 = 12	3 × 6 = 18		

TIMES-TABLES GAME 30

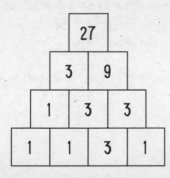

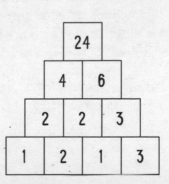

TIMES-TABLES GAME 31

	4	6	6	4	
12	4	3	2	1	2
2	1	2	3	4	12
2	2	1	4	3	12
12	3	4	1	2	2
	6	4	4	6	

TIMES-TABLES GAME 32

a) The garden is 5 x 4 = 20 m² in area. If three-quarters is grassed over, then the grassed-over area is 15 m² in area. The only way to form this using a whole number of metres in each dimension is for the grassed-over area to be **5 m wide by 3 m in length**. (It can't be 3 m wide by 5 m in length, because the garden is only 4 m in length to start with).

b) She cut the biscuits in half once to get 8 pieces, and then in half again to get **16 pieces**.

TIMES-TABLES GAME 33

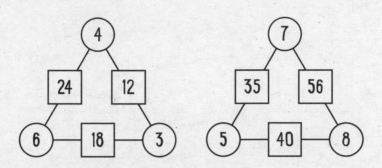

TIMES-TABLES GAME 34

$33 = 11 \times 3$

$56 = 8 \times 7$

$132 = 11 \times 12$

TIMES-TABLES GAME 35

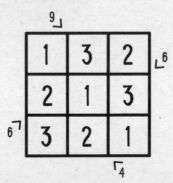

TIMES-TABLES GAME 36

A fish

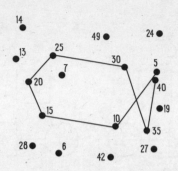

TIMES-TABLES GAME 37

A = 1, B = 2, C = 3,
giving 12 x 11 = 132
and 3 x 7 = 21.

TIMES-TABLES GAME 38

The product is 48
(2 x 4 x 3 x 2 x 1).

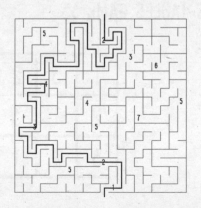

TIMES-TABLES GAME 39

The 9 m² square has dimensions of 3 m x 3 m, and the 16 m² square has dimensions of 4 m x 4 m. This means that the largest square must have dimensions of (3 m + 4 m) x (3 m + 4 m) = 7 m x 7 m = 49 m².

TIMES-TABLES GAME 40

a) $3 \times 12 \div 6 \times 9 = 54$

b) $7 \times 8 - 2 \div 9 = 6$

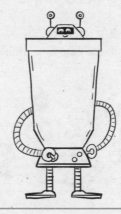

TIMES-TABLES GAME 41

 = 5

 = 6

 = 2

TIMES-TABLES GAME 42

a) After cutting the bananas the first time she has 9 pieces, and after cutting them again she now has **27 pieces**.

b) The children are **3, 4** and **6** years old.

TIMES-TABLES GAME 43

The digit is '5', to give 45, 55, 25, 50, 35 and 15. These are all multiples in the five times table.

TIMES-TABLES GAME 44

8 4	1	2	6 3
3	12 4	4 1	2
2 2	3	4	1
1	24 2	3	4

48 3	4	2 2	1
4	1	6 3	2
6 2	3	1	48 4
2 1	2	4	3

TIMES-TABLES GAME 45

5	10	15	20
6	12	18	24
7	14	21	28
8	16	24	32

TIMES-TABLES GAME 46

6	×	7	=	42
×	■	×		
8	×	4	=	32
=		=		
48		28		

TIMES-TABLES GAME 47

a) Burst 4, 6. 8. 9 and 3 to leave 2 x 10 = 20

b) Burst 4, 2. 6. 8 and 10 to leave 9 x 3 = 27

c) Burst 2, 6. 10. 9 and 3 to leave 4 x 8 = 32

d) Burst 6. 10. 9 and 3 to leave 2 x 4 x 8 = 64

TIMES-TABLES GAME 48

	45	21	21	45	
15	5	3	7	9	63
63	9	7	3	5	15
35	7	5	9	3	27
27	3	9	5	7	35
	21	45	45	21	

TIMES-TABLES GAME 49

a) 3 times table and 4 times table: 3 4 6 8 9 12 15 16 18

b) 4 times table and 5 times table: 4 5 8 10 12 15 16 20 24

c) 3 times table and 7 times table: 3 6 7 9 12 14 15 18 21

d) 4 times table and 6 times table: 4 6 8 12 16 18 20 24 28

TIMES-TABLES GAME 50

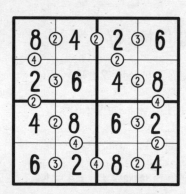

TIMES-TABLES GAME 51

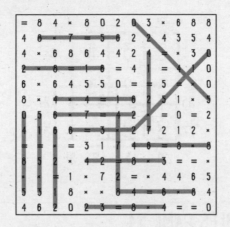

4 × 7 = 28	3 × 5 = 15	5 × 4 = 20	7 × 2 = 14
2 × 3 = 6	3 × 8 = 24	5 × 8 = 40	8 × 6 = 48
2 × 5 = 10	4 × 4 = 16	6 × 2 = 12	8 × 7 = 56
2 × 8 = 16	4 × 8 = 32	6 × 7 = 42	8 × 8 = 64

TIMES-TABLES GAME 52

A boat

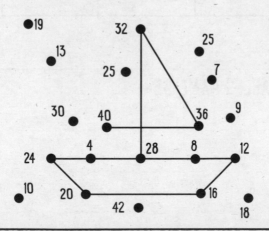

TIMES-TABLES GAME 53

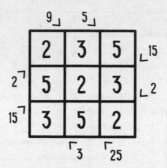

TIMES-TABLES GAME 54

Two Multiples of 4	Two Multiples of 6	Two Multiples of 8
20	12	16
44	30	24

TIMES-TABLES GAME 55

$48 = 2 \times 4 \times 6$

$64 = 2 \times 4 \times 8$

$132 = 2 \times 11 \times 6$

TIMES-TABLES GAME 56

= 3

= 8

= 2

= 4

TIMES-TABLES GAME 57

$3 \times 6 = 18$ $6 \times 5 = 30$ $8 \times 9 = 72$
(example)

$4 \times 7 = 28$ $9 \times 4 = 36$

TIMES-TABLES GAME 58

5	3 ②	6	③ 2	② 4	④ 1
	③				③
2 ②	1	④ 4	5	6	② 3
②	⑤			⑥	
4	5	3 ②	6	⑥ 1	② 2
		③		③	
6	③ 2	② 1	④ 4	3	5
②	②	②	④		
3	4 ②	2	② 1	⑤ 5	6
③			③		
1	⑥ 6	5	3	2	② 4

TIMES-TABLES GAME 59

28	32	36	40
35	40	45	50
42	48	54	60
49	56	63	70

TIMES-TABLES GAME 60

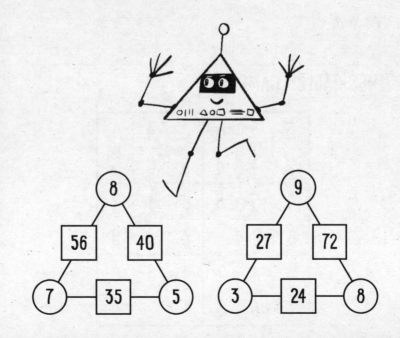

TIMES-TABLES GAME 61

		5	×	3	=	15
		×	■	×		
4	×	2	×	6	=	48
×	■	×	■	×		
8	×	7	×	1	=	56
=		=		=		
32		70		18		

TIMES-TABLES GAME 62

Left grid:

[4] 4	1	[6] 2	3
[2] 2	[12] 3	4	[2] 1
1	[12] 4	3	2
[6] 3	2	[4] 1	4

Right grid:

[8] 4	[6] 3	[8] 2	1
2	1	[12] 3	4
[12] 1	2	4	[6] 3
3	4	1	2

TIMES-TABLES GAME 63

a) 9 x 9 – 1 ÷ 10 x 7 = 56

b) 7 x 5 + 1 ÷ 6 x 11 = 66

TIMES-TABLES GAME 64

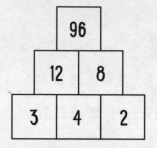 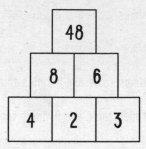

TIMES-TABLES GAME 65

	6	4	30	4	10	18	
48	2	4	6	1	5	3	15
15	3	1	5	4	2	6	48
12	1	6	2	5	3	4	60
60	5	3	4	2	6	1	12
12	6	2	1	3	4	5	60
60	4	5	3	6	1	2	12
	24	10	3	18	4	10	

TIMES-TABLES GAME 66

a) 7 x 1 x 6 = 42

b) 10 x 1 x 12 = 120

c) 3 x 6 x 2 = 36

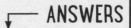
TIMES-TABLES GAME 67

a) 3 times table and 8 times table: 3 6 8 9 12 15 16 18 21

b) 4 times table and 7 times table: 4 7 8 12 14 16 20 21 24

c) 5 times table and 6 times table: 5 6 10 12 15 18 20 24 25

d) 4 times table and 9 times table: 4 8 9 12 16 18 20 24 27

TIMES-TABLES GAME 68

The digit is '3', to give 32, 63, 36, 35, 30 and 33. One way to form these results is from 4 x 8, 9 x 7, 6 x 6, 7 x 5, 5 x 6 and 3 x 11, respectively.

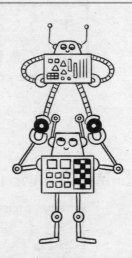

TIMES-TABLES GAME 69

a) With ten bottles in each box, if three are broken then seven remain. With seven per box, and two sets of five boxes, he has 7 x 2 x 5 = **70 bottles** out for sale.

b) The only way to make 99 by multiplying three different numbers under 12 is with 1 x 9 x 11, so the children must be **1, 9 and 11** years old.

TIMES-TABLES GAME 70

2	9 ③	3	③ 1	⑦ 7	8
②			②		
1	⑧ 8	7	2	9 ③	3
③	⑧				
3 ③	1 ⑧	8	9	2	7
	②				⑦
7	2	9	8	3 ③	1
				③	⑨
8	3	2	7 ⑦	1 ⑨	9
		②		⑧	
9	7 ⑦	1 ③	3	8 ④	2

TIMES-TABLES GAME 71

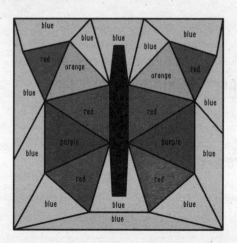

TIMES-TABLES GAME 72

a) Burst 4, 10, 5, 8 and 2 to leave 3 x 6 = 18

b) Burst 4, 10, 5 and 8 to leave 2 x 3 x 6 = 36

c) Burst 6, 10, 3 and 5 to leave 2 x 4 x 8 = 64

d) Burst 10, 5, 8 and 2 to leave 3 x 4 x 6 = 72

e) Burst 4, 6, 3 and 8 to leave 2 x 5 x 10 = 100

TIMES-TABLES GAME 73

A ghost

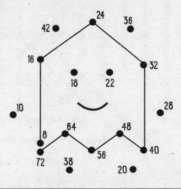

TIMES-TABLES GAME 74

2	12	4	
2	3	4	1
1	4	2 (6)	3
4 (4)	1	3 (3)	2 (8)
3 (6)	2	1	4

6		72	2
3	2	4	1
1 (12)	4	3	2
4 (8)	1	2	3
2	3	1 (4)	4

TIMES-TABLES GAME 75

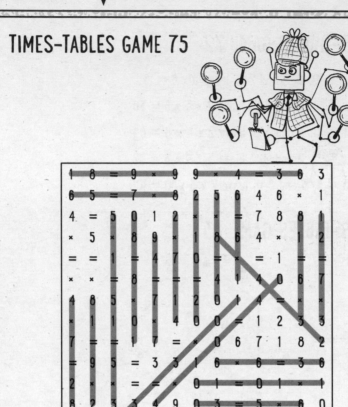

1	8	=	9	9	9	×	4	=	3	6	3
6	5	=	7	×	8	2	5	6	4	6	×	1
4	=	5	0	1	2	×	=	7	8	8	1
×	5	×	8	9	×	1	8	6	4	×	1	2
=	=	1	=	4	7	0	=	=	1	=
×	×	=	8	=	=	×	4	1	4	0	6	7
4	8	5	×	7	1	2	0	1	4	=
×	1	1	0	×	4	0	0	=	1	2	3	3
7	=	0	1	7	=	×	0	6	7	1	8	2
=	9	5	=	3	3	1	6	×	6	=	3	6
2	×	=	=	=	4	0	1	=	0	1	×	1
8	2	3	3	4	9	0	3	=	5	×	6	0
1	5	0	4	3	7	=	1	×	7	1	×	×

1 × 10 = 10	4 × 7 = 28	8 × 4 = 32
1 × 6 = 6	4 × 10 = 40	8 × 7 = 56
2 × 7 = 14	5 × 1 = 5	9 × 4 = 36
2 × 9 = 18	5 × 8 = 40	9 × 9 = 81
2 × 10 = 20	6 × 5 = 30	10 × 3 = 30
3 × 5 = 15	6 × 6 = 36	10 × 8 = 80
3 × 6 = 18	7 × 1 = 7	
3 × 7 = 21	7 × 7 = 49	

TIMES-TABLES GAME 76

= 7

= 6

= 8

= 9

TIMES-TABLES GAME 77

63	72	81	90
70	80	90	100
77	88	99	110
84	96	108	120

TIMES-TABLES GAME 78

	24⌐	8⌐		
	3	4	2	1	⌐4
	1	2	3	4	⌐8
4⌐	4	3	1	2	
16⌐| 2	1	4	3	
			⌐4	⌐12|

TIMES-TABLES GAME 79

Two Multiples of 6	Two Multiples of 8	Two Multiples of 12
18	16	36
30	48	60

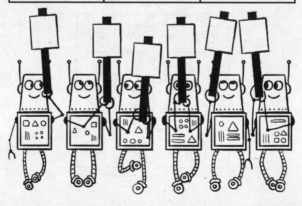

TIMES-TABLES GAME 80

5	1	4	6	3	2
6	3	2	1	5	4
2	5	6	3	4	1
3	4	1	5	2	6
4	6	3	2	1	5
1	2	5	4	6	3

TIMES-TABLES GAME 81

The product is 24
(4 x 2 x 1 x 3 x 1).

TIMES-TABLES GAME 82

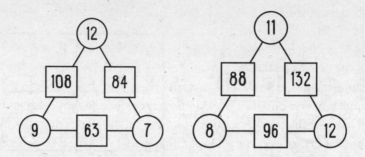

TIMES-TABLES GAME 83

30		2		24	36
6	5	2	1	4	3
24		20 ×			
3	1	4	5	6	2
		30	6		
2	4	5	3	1	6
20	36			40	
1	3	6	2	5	4
		12			
5	6	3	4	2	1
		6		15	
4	2	1	6	3	5

TIMES-TABLES GAME 84

$12 = 3 \times 2 \times 2$

$40 = 4 \times 5 \times 2$

$54 = 3 \times 2 \times 9$

TIMES-TABLES GAME 85

The two grey rectangles each have the same width and height, so the two dotted squares must each be the same size. This means that the area of one grey rectangle and dotted square is 44 cm². You can see that the square and rectangle have the same height, so you can now experiment with different heights until you find one that works – or you can notice that 44 is in the 11 times table, which suggests that the square and rectangle are each 4 cm tall. With a 7x4 rectangle and a 4x4 square, you do indeed have an area of 28 + 16 = 44 cm². Therefore the square is 4 cm x 4 cm, giving it an area of **16 cm²**.

TIMES-TABLES GAME 86

TIMES-TABLES GAME 87

a) 6 times table and 7 times table: 6 7 12 14 18 21 24 28 30

b) 5 times table and 8 times table: 5 8 10 15 16 20 24 25 30

c) 7 times table and 8 times table: 7 8 14 16 21 24 28 32 35

d) 9 times table and 11 times table: 9 11 18 22 27 33 36 44 45

TIMES-TABLES GAME 88

A cube

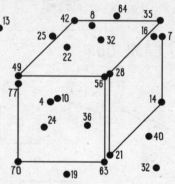

TIMES-TABLES GAME 89

$5 \times 8 = 40$

$7 \times 5 = 35$ (example)

$8 \times 6 = 48$

$9 \times 7 = 63$

$12 \times 9 = 108$

TIMES-TABLES GAME 90

a) 5 x 3 x 4 = 60

b) 7 x 8 = 56

c) 2 x 3 x 3 = 18

TIMES-TABLES GAME 91

The digit is '6', to give 36, 64, 16, 60, 96 and 56. One way to form these results is from 6 x 6, 8 x 8, 8 x 2, 6 x 10, 8 x 12 and 7 x 8.

TIMES-TABLES GAME 92

	10	3	24	30	2	12	
36	2	3	6	5	1	4	20
20	5	1	4	6	2	3	36
30	3	5	2	4	6	1	24
24	4	6	1	3	5	2	30
36	6	2	3	1	4	5	20
20	1	4	5	2	3	6	36
	6	8	15	2	12	30	

TIMES-TABLES GAME 93

a) Burst 4. 9. 11, 8 and 5 to leave 2 x 12 = 24

b) Burst 9, 11. 5 and 12 to leave 2 x 4 x 8 = 64

c) Burst 4. 9. 11 and 12 to leave 2 x 5 x 8 = 80

d) Burst 4. 9. 2. 8 and 5 to leave 11 x 12 = 132

TIMES-TABLES GAME 94

1	×	5	×	6	=	30
×	■	×	■	×		
9	×	2	×	4	=	72
×	■	×	■	=		
3	×	8	=	24		
=		=				
27		80				

TIMES-TABLES GAME 95

54	60	66	72
63	70	77	84
72	80	88	96
81	90	99	108

TIMES-TABLES GAME 96

Left grid:

24 3	2	4	6 1
4 1	4	2	3
8 2	1	12 3	4
4	6 3	1	2

Right grid:

72 3	4	2	6 1
8 1	3	4	2
4	2	12 1	3
2	1	3	4

TIMES-TABLES GAME 97

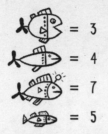 = 3

= 4

= 7

= 5

TIMES-TABLES GAME 98

a) 12 x 7 + 4 ÷ 8 x 11 = 121

b) 3 x 4 x 12 – 24 ÷ 10 = 12

TIMES-TABLES GAME 99

4	10	12	6	2	8
8	6	2	12	4	10
10	12	4	8	6	2
2	8	6	4	10	12
12	4	10	2	8	6
6	2	8	10	12	4

TIMES-TABLES GAME 100

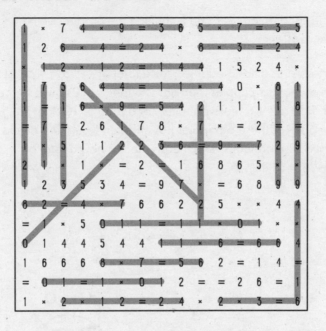

11 × 11 = 121	4 × 4 = 16	6 × 12 = 72	9 × 9 = 81
1 × 7 = 7	4 × 9 = 36	7 × 4 = 28	10 × 1 = 10
2 × 3 = 6	4 × 11 = 44	7 × 9 = 63	10 × 11 = 110
2 × 5 = 10	5 × 7 = 35	8 × 3 = 24	11 × 6 = 66
2 × 12 = 24	6 × 4 = 24	8 × 7 = 56	12 × 6 = 72
3 × 5 = 15	6 × 9 = 54	9 × 2 = 18	12 × 12 = 144

TIMES-TABLES GAME 101

a) The children are **3**, **4** and **5**, making the product of their ages equal to **60**.

b) The first dog has 3 puppies, for a total of 1 + 3 = 4 dogs. Each of those 3 puppies then has 2 puppies of its own, so there are now 3 x 2 = 6 more puppies, for a total of 10 dogs. Then each of those 6 puppies has another 4 puppies, giving 6 x 4 = 24 more dogs. This means there is now a total of 10 + 24 = **34 dogs**.

The end!

Well done

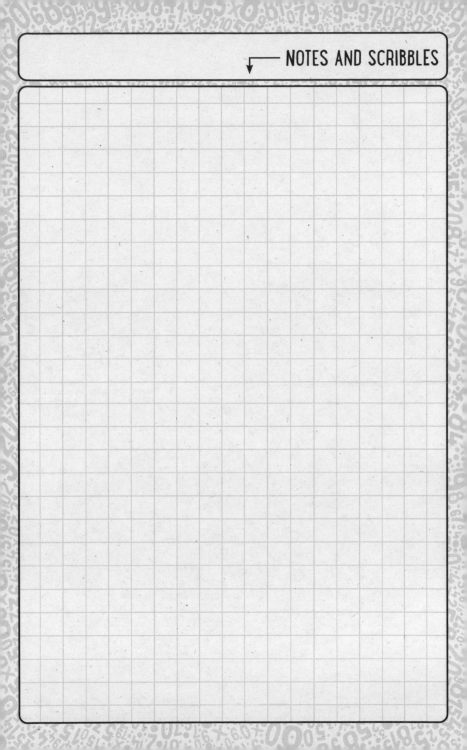

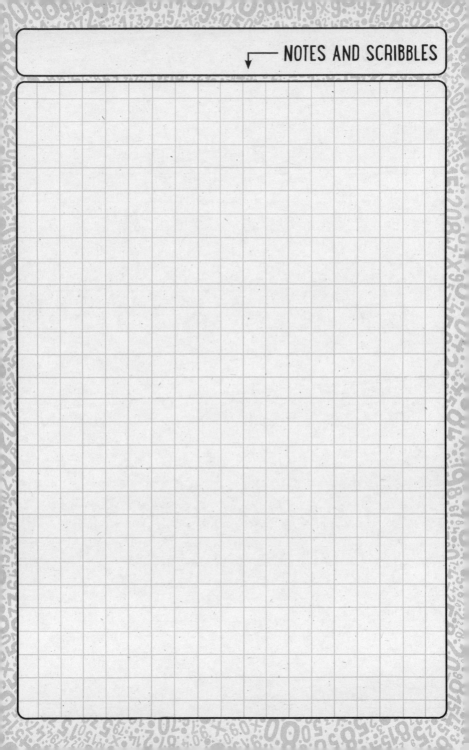

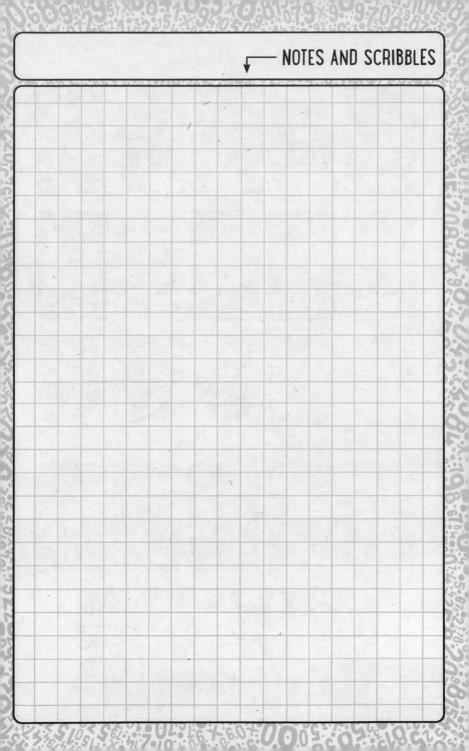

ALSO AVAILABLE:

ISBN 9781780558882   ISBN 9781780559155   ISBN 9781780558738   ISBN 9781780558264   ISBN 9781780558721

ISBN 9781780557403   ISBN 9781780557106   ISBN 9781780556642   ISBN 9781780556635   ISBN 9781780556628

ISBN 9781780556543   ISBN 9781780556659   ISBN 9781780556192   ISBN 9781780556208   ISBN 9781780556185

ISBN 9781780555935   ISBN 9781780555638   ISBN 9781780554730   ISBN 9781780554723   ISBN 9781780555409

ISBN 9781780553146   ISBN 9781780553085   ISBN 9781780553078   ISBN 9781780552491